Laredo

Memoirs of My Home Town

by

Deacon José Guadalupe Díaz

San Antonio, 2013

A *Watercress Press* book
from Geron & Associates
www. watercresspress.com

ISBN-13: 978-0934955-317

Dedication

To my lovely wife, María Yolanda . . . thank you for your goodness and your generosity.

Thank you for your love and prayers, and thank you, of course, for the delicious coffee cakes.

Contents

Laredo

Memoirs of My Home Town

Preface

This is not a masterpiece. I never had the time to write one. This is a collection of notes jotted down from time to time to present to you a noble but a simple story about my beloved "brush country" and my hometown of Laredo, Texas.

And just what is a masterpiece? Experts tell us that a masterpiece is a work done with extraordinary skill and a supreme intellectual or artistic achievement. Wow! That leaves me out! To me, the greatest masterpiece written by William Shakespeare is *The Tempest*. This is one of my favorite works of Shakespeare and as I get older I've grown to appreciate it more and more. This is a tragic story of madness and laughter. Also, being an amateur oil painter myself, I consider *The Water Lilies* as the greatest masterpiece by French artist Claude Monet.

However, while *Laredo – Memoirs of my Home Town* might not be a masterpiece, you will find a beautiful story of love, humility, hard times, and resilience. Of course, as you read it, I hope you will let out a chuckle or two or even a hearty laugh. Beginning with my childhood, I include my school days, a bit of Laredo's history and its politics, my life in sports, my military duty, and finally, my complete surrender to the Creator, and my ordination to the Sacred Order of Deacon. I promise . . . you will enjoy the journey.

Chapter 1 – Childhood and Early Beginnings

I was a child of the Great Depression. Times were hard and difficult. It began with the crash of the stock market in October 1929, and rapidly spread throughout the country. Families had no money to buy food. Unemployment was at a record high and there were bread lines and soup lines in many of the big cities. The banks went broke and people were losing their homes. Millions of Americans were in fear of what would happen next. Things did not look well.

In his inauguration speech President Franklin D. Roosevelt delivered some very convincing words to a country that was in despair and fear. President Roosevelt called for faith in the future of America when he said: *"The only thing we have to fear is fear itself."* Just what is fear? Sacred Scripture contains many passages which pertain to fear. Do you know that many of us live in fear? We fear sickness, suffering, and failure. Do you know that many people in this world are not only afraid to die, but they are afraid to live? Really, let's face it; if you fear, you are afraid. And you know what? Either fear will conquer you or you will conquer fear. If you learn to control fear, you will be blessed and if you cannot control fear it will defeat you. *"God is our refuge and our strength, an ever-present help in distress. Therefore, we will not fear."* (Psalm 46:2-3)

The Great Depression also brought anxiety and concern to my hometown of Laredo, Texas. But, let me say this; with all the tumult and unrest, with all of the ugly things that were happening because of the suffering and poverty in the Laredo area, believe me, there was some hope. There was hope and optimism in our humble residence in the 2400 block of San Darío Avenue in Laredo. My father was

Guadalupe F. Díaz, and my mother was Francisca Gutierrez Díaz. My wonderful and special mother was a thin and fragile woman who already suffered from the early symptoms of tuberculosis. But this beautiful woman, a human dynamo, was also a courageous woman of great faith and hope.

When I was a boy of about six years old, my mother said these inspiring and reassuring words that I have never forgotten. She said: *"Dios nos ayudará, no hay que temer, tenemos que tener fe en El."* *"God will help us, there is no need to fear, we need to have faith in Him."*

My journey now begins . . .

1934 – My brother Jesse standing, I am sitting.

Chapter 2 – My Father and My Mother

The years 1910 to 1920 are considered the most violent and turbulent period in Mexican history. Angry and frustrated at the regime of President Porfirio Díaz, the citizens united to overthrow his presidency. The Revolution began and brought many immigrants to Laredo. My father and mother were part of that great migration north to escape the blood and the civil war in their country. Immigrants looked to the United States to find employment and better opportunities. Many who came to Laredo found work primarily in railroad construction, maintenance, and agriculture.

My father found employment with the International and Great Northern Railroad, later the Missouri Pacific Railroad. After that, Dad built and started his general store on San Darío Street. With this employment and the companionship of his good wife, my mother, eight children were raised. He was a good father and a hard worker even with the few opportunities he had in his life. However, Dad had that great drive and purpose to provide for the betterment of his children. In my daily prayers I have always thanked God for Dad's sacrifices and for the love and generosity he showed to all of us. Additionally, in my prayers I also included the "tough love" and discipline that my father made available to me. No doubt about it, I needed it and it worked.

Someone once said that a good father is one who is forced to endure childbirth without an anesthetic. A good father gives when he can give no more. A good father cares, and he disciplines. A father teaches, and by his example we learn. A father can be tough and strong but he can be tender and loving, especially when he sees his children take their first steps or when their children bring home good grades from school. As I was growing up I could see how my father worked and struggled, and I often wondered how he made ends meet with so many children to feed.

I honestly believe that to be a father is one of the great and noble privileges that a man can have. To be a father is to be a companion of God. It is important to remember that our character and most of our own values were formed by our father. No matter how humble and lowly his work is, no matter his position in life, a good father will always leave a lasting impression on his family. *"Honor your father and your mother,"* reads the 4th Commandment of God, *"so that you may be happy and you may have a long life."* (Exodus 20: 12) What does it mean to honor someone? It means to treat him with respect, not because he is perfect but because God has given him a special place in your life. Even if my dad used a belt to take me to school, I loved him for that. It worked and it was necessary for that little brat and expert rock thrower (*piedrero*) from the streets of Laredo. You only have one father, and in spite of his faults, God gave Him to you – and he gave you to him.

My dad was called by his Creator on the 7th of January 1989. On the 10th of January, I performed the graveside service and assisted at the altar during the funeral mass. The following is part of the homily that I preached about Dad:

When you live a long life it is often considered a sign of God's favor. (My dad lived to pass 100 years old.) Our Jewish forefathers in the Old Testament looked upon old age as a special blessing from Yahweh, and in the book of Proverbs God tells us: *"Gray hair is a crown of glory; it is gained by virtuous living."* (Proverbs 16: 31) This morning we mourn the death of my father but at the same time we praise God for allowing him to live a long life. Our hearts today are sad, and we are hurting – it is also hurting for me as I proclaim this homily. But at the same time our heavy hearts are enlightened today by the sure knowledge that our beloved *Viejito* has found favor with the Lord and most of all I am reassured that he is now at peace with his Maker. For those of you present here that didn't know my dad, let me say that he was a simple man, not a man of material wealth, though whatever he had, he shared. His education was limited, but he was gifted with that God-given virtue of wisdom. My dad in his wisdom could enjoy the beauty of the stars, a beautiful sunrise or sunset. He could not explain to you however, the intricate and complex details of the universe, the galaxies, the Milky Way or the constellations. But in admiring the universe, the sunrise, and the sunset, he knew it was God's creation. And my dad knew that a creation demands a creator, and that creator is Almighty God. That same creator, he would say, is ruler and king and in charge of this earth, and not a political or any military leader.

But most important my dad knew that at an appointed time, you and I would render an account of our selves to that creator God. He is doing that right now. Saint Paul tells us that our lives are similar to a race. We begin at the starting line the day we are born and finish the race the day we die. However, Paul insists that we look to the finish line, to press forward, and if we fall, to get up and fight the good fight and finish the race. And when we finish the race a grand prize is awaiting us.

And just what is that prize? The prize is a calling from the Lord. I can just see my dad in God's holy throne in all his humility, yet with that ever witty smile accepting the prize – the calling: Well done, good and faithful servant, you have fought a good fight, you have kept the faith, you have finished the race. Come now, blessed of my Father, and receive the prize, the Kingdom prepared for you from the foundation of the world. Come share the joy of eternal happiness with the Lord, forever and ever. Amen.

Just like Dad, I dearly loved my mother. They say that most of the beautiful things in life come in pairs, or in dozens, or in the hundreds or thousands. For example, a pair of carnations, a dozen roses, hundreds of beautiful bluebonnets in the fields of South Texas, or thousands of pretty shiny stars in the sky. Most of you have many uncles, aunts, *padrinos,* and *compadres*. But throughout the whole world, there is only one mother. The good Lord blessed me with that mother, a godly mother. In my mind and in the minds of men there are no sweeter memories than that of a good mother. I believe that the voice of a mother can calm the fear of a child. It is a mother's touch that can relieve most pains. It was the presence of my mother that gave me an unshakable confidence. My mother cared for me when I was helpless, and she watched over me like a guardian angel. A good mother will love you even in times when you are unlovable.

I really believe that a good mother is the best picture of God that some of us will ever know. We all remember our mothers – we should. One of the earliest memories of my mother was her insistence; she made me to go to school and church. My mother never gave up on me, even in those hard and difficult times of my childhood years. My mother still carried that Christ-like hope and faith that things would go well with me in my education. As it turned out. I eventually went on to college and the seminary. Many times I have asked myself; what happened to that little self-centered brat and bully who didn't care for church or school? The prayers of a righteous mother sure work in miraculous ways. How accurate then is one of my favorite Bible passages: *"She speaks with a wisdom and her tongue is a kindly counsel."* (Proverbs 31: 26)

As my mother struggled through the last years of her earthly life, she told me something that I have never forgotten. One morning at the nursing home, as I held her hands, those lovely hands that had aged with time and hard work, but somehow were still tender and affectionate, she told me that it wasn't just only the spankings from my dad that changed me, but she felt that her constant prayers also helped. I have always believed in answered prayer but be certain and guaranteed that Almighty God always answers the prayers of a *good* mother. These then, are my treasured memories of my mother, and these memories come alive as I pray to her my morning prayers of the Liturgy of the Hours. My mother's life was full of love, caring, and sacrifice and she was always a great source of inspiration to me. Oh yes, before I forget, there's one thing more Mom used to tell me because I got up so early in the morning. (And I still do.) She would tell me: *"Mijo tu hubieras sido un panadero o un monje."* "You should have been a baker or a monk."

Twenty-five years after her death, I can gladly say: "Mom, I truly thank you; I appreciate all that you did for me, and I acknowledge your goodness and sincerity." I am so lucky and blessed because my loving God loaned me (just for a while) one of His most precious jewels . . . my mother. She was my Mom and my dearest friend. Sadly I write the final words of this chapter but I also feel so grateful and thankful for Mom's answered prayers. Thanks again, Lord, for giving me a wonderful mother. Truly, my mother's life has given me a picture of God that I could have received nowhere else on earth. Then, as if this was not enough of a blessing for me, I have been privileged to see a picture of my mother in one who was my wife for 43 years. With a like grace and blessing, my wife was also a good and a godly mother to our children. How blest I am! And so, for a wonderful Mom and Dad . . . *Muchas Gracias Eterno Dios.*

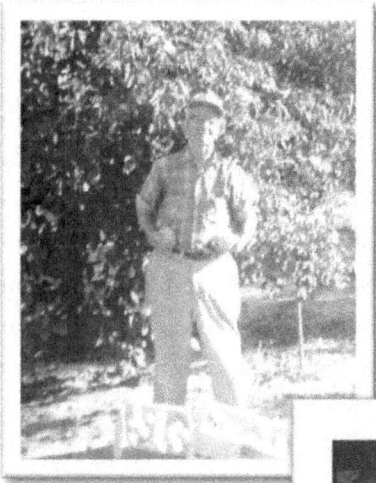

Dad proudly showing his oranges.

Mom, Dad, and my Cousin Elvira.

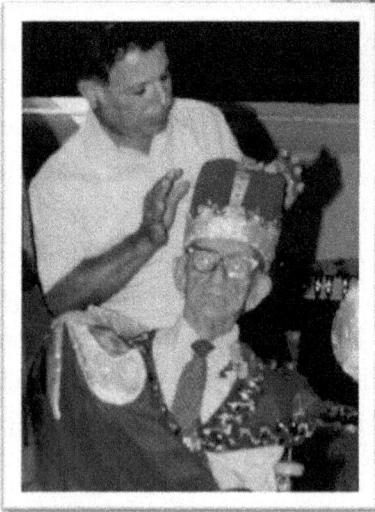

Dad on his 100th birthday.

Chapter 3 – My Home and My First School – Bruni Elementary

My home was located on the corner of San Darío Avenue and Shea Street. We were only two blocks from San Bernardo Avenue, formerly U.S. Highway 81, which stretched all the way to Canada. Now it is adjacent to IH 35. The noted Zacate Creek was only a few blocks to the east, and Bruni Elementary School was a half-mile south. The house and my dad's grocery store were the same structure. My best estimation is that the house was built around 1927, give or take a few years. The area was still not all populated. Whatever streets there were, were not paved, and there was brush, mesquite, and cactus surrounding much of the vicinity. Even the vast *Colonia de Guadalupe* was not built yet.

As mentioned before, the house and store were all one. It was big, sturdy, and well-constructed. The house consisted of three bedrooms with old-fashioned high ceilings, a kitchen, a small dining room, and a small bathroom. I said bathroom, not toilet. The privy was approximately forty-five feet away from the house, beyond the orange trees. By the way, the outhouse was a two-seater and by all means, newspapers were available but not the traditional old Sears & Roebuck catalog.

There was a hall from the store which went past two of the bedrooms and led to the back porch. What a dazzling and beautiful site was the porch or the *galería*! As I reflect now, more than seventy years later, I still remember the beauty and serenity of that porch. There were lounge chairs and room to sit by the edge of the porch, and it was surrounded by a flower bed. On the east side of the porch facing the orange and peach trees was a huge scarlet bougainvillea plant. This was the ideal place to sit and relax during the hot *canícula*, the dog days of summer. Many times I often wondered just how in the world my parents found the time to maintain such a beautiful porch. My father was always busy in the store, and my mother had all the chores of a home, children to take care of, washing, ironing, cooking, and so on. Maybe the weather was hot and humid, but that porch always seemed to me like a quiet and peaceful place. As I grew older I referred to this porch as the barrio's "Garden of Eden." It was a lovely site and I always cherished it.

It seems that most of the country knows that Laredo is a hot spot. As I traveled the fifty states of America, Canada, and Mexico, numerous people would ask me about the fiery weather in Laredo. As a result, many yarns, wisecracks, and jokes have developed due to the hot and scorching weather of my hometown. Here's a few of them:

It gets so hot in Laredo that the Brinks armored trucks have screen doors.

It was so hot in Laredo that Satan decided to take the day off.

I was playing golf in Laredo's Casablanca golf course when I saw a coyote chasing a rabbit . . . and it was so hot that both of them were walking.

It gets so hot in Laredo that fire hydrants chase the dogs.

And I can go on and on . . .

Oh yes, we had a telephone in the house. At this time the majority of homes in the neighborhood did not have a phone. We had a phone not because we were prosperous or affluent, but the phone was needed for my dad's business. The phone was located in the house and not in the store. Why? Because if it was in the store it was considered commercial and the monthly bill was higher. It was a black bulky telephone on the wall of the hall leading to the porch. It was the old-fashioned kind where you didn't dial – you talked to the operator and gave her the number you wanted. There were diverse and varied uses for the famous phone. Generally, the most important use of that instrument was when Dad would call the wholesalers to order the needed supplies to replenish his inventory. Ranchers would also call Dad on the phone to give him a list of the necessary items that they needed. He made frequent delivery trips to the nearby ranches in his 1936 Model T pick-up truck. In some instances I would tag along for the ride. I enjoyed the brush country.

However the phone was also used for various and sundry reasons and situations. In times of emergency and in the middle of the night, mothers and fathers would come to use the phone to call the doctor. Frequently at night we could hear the knocking on the porch door as people asked to use the phone. It was also true that after the store closed for the evening, there was again knocking at the porch door and Dad would sell whatever over-the-counter medicine they needed. How generous and considerate a man was my dad for helping his neighbors! As a youngster I often wondered why he had to do this. *"Amen, I say to you, whatever you did for one of these least of my brothers, you did it for me."* (Matthew 25: 40)

But "Holy Moses" and *"hijo de la fregada,"* there was an additional use for that renowned phone. It was known as *el chisme* or gossip. Young men and women, as well as the not-too-young, would come to use the phone for amorous and passionate conversations. Oh Lord, love-making by telephone. They were the boyfriends and girlfriends, lovers, sweethearts of that era. In San Antonio they call it *"La Movida."* Enough said about the adorable *teléfono*.

Finally, Bruni School; when I was six years old, Bruni Elementary was my first school. Each time I visit Laredo I always drive by Bruni to reminisce about my first school days, long ago. However, I have to be honest and admit that there is another reason I go by Bruni School. My other concern is to stop at the nearby Superior Bakery or *panadería* on San Eduardo Street and buy four of those

famous and delicious *semitas* (pastries). As I look at the remodeled
Bruni School I recall my first education years as well as my
achievements and youthful dreams. You went to Bruni School from
the 1st to the 5th grade. After that, you went to Katherine Tarver
School in downtown Laredo for the 6th grade, then to L. J. Christen
School for the 7th and 8th grade and finally to the 9th through 12th
grades at Martin High School.

How well I remember some of my teachers at Bruni: Mrs. Cruz
and Mrs. Bunn were my favorites. Actually, Mrs. Bunn was a
commuter teacher. She also went to other schools to play the piano
for the children. I was especially fond of those patriotic songs that we
sang along as she played the piano. The Second World War had
started against Germany. In view of this, the theme songs for the
Army, Navy, and Marines were very popular. Another item of
patriotism was that if the weather permitted, the student body would
recite the pledge of allegiance by the flagpole.

However, there were some firsts for me at Bruni School.

- I was in the first fight of my life . . . really, just a shoving match.
  (Shame, shame, Deacon Díaz!) The scene of the fight was under
  a tree on the north side of the Bruni campus. By the way, that tree
  is still there. It was the general agreement or consensus of those
  kids watching that I lost the quarrel which only lasted a whole
  minute. Later we shook hands; big deal.
- She was a pretty six-year-old girl who was in the first grade at
  Bruni School with me. There were about twenty kids in the first
  grade and she sat right in front of me. Her name was María
  Yolanda – my future wife.
- It was at Bruni where I first went to a theater to see a movie. Two
  or three weeks before the end of the school year, the tradition was
  that two or three classes of Bruni students, accompanied by their
  teachers, would walk to the Royal Theater in downtown Laredo

to see a movie . . . a Western. Perhaps some of you have not heard of those gallant and daring cowboy dudes of yesteryear: Hopalong Cassidy, Johnny Mack Brown, Gene Autry, Tex Ritter, and others. These guys were the real heroes of that generation. In the cantina fistfights with the outlaws the white cowboy hat of the good guy never came off and their six-shooters carried 37 rounds of ammunition. At the end of the movie the hero cowboy would kiss his horse (not the dame) and ride away into the sunset. End of movie. After that, there was tremendous applause from all the Bruni School students. As always, the good guy with the white hat was the victor. Yippee!

- It was also at Bruni School where I first went through a series of inoculations. All children were vaccinated for protection against smallpox and other ailments. During my days on this earth I have never been very charmed or fond of vaccinations, inoculations, and the rest. I can't stand them – I hate them and I still do my best to avoid them. At this time, my recollection is vivid as I remember the second time I went to Korea. Assigned to my second aircraft carrier *USS Antietam*, I witnessed the largest inoculation project that I have ever seen. After crossing the International Date Line, the project got underway. On the hangar deck and in groups of over 200 sailors at one time, pants down, we received four types of vaccinations, one on each arm, and one on each rear cheek. And you're darn tooting, those shots hurt and I have never forgotten it. Don't ever remind me of needles and vaccinations, O.K.?

- It was a first at Bruni that all students were checked or examined for head lice. (*Piojos*) This was embarrassing, but at the same time humorous. If they found lice in your hair you were sent home with a yellow paper warning your parents and at the same time advising them how to treat you for lice. To those children who received the yellow paper you could hear the consistent phrase addressed to them by their classmates: *Piojoso* or *Piojosa*.

Finally, in my account of Bruni Elementary School, I left the best for the last. There were many times that I just didn't want to go to school or to church. At that young age, I felt that school and church were not my piece of cake. Oh, really – how nice! But let me assure you that my father wanted me to go to church and school. And guess who won? Dad was not an educated man, as he only had a third- or fourth-grade education. He was a hard-working man but a man gifted with wisdom. Bear in mind that you do not acquire wisdom at a university or a seminary. Wisdom is a God-given gift where you will learn and understand goodness from evil and light from darkness. If you want wisdom, you ask God and He will give you wisdom. *"But if any one of you lacks wisdom, let him ask it from God, and it will be given to him."* (James 1:5)

So, how about that; I didn't care to go to school or church! In that case Dad used wisdom. It was called a belt. Years ago, a belt was not only used to hold up your pants but to administer wisdom. You know what? Little by little I started liking school and church. After their marriage, my two daughters reminded me often as they told me: "Dad, aren't you embarrassed to tell people in your homilies and Bible classes that Grandpa got after you with a belt?" Well, not really; it happened, it is the truth, and it worked. Shirley, my youngest daughter, is a school principal in Fort Worth, and I know she is a strict disciplinarian and I am sure she understands the necessity for discipline.

And so by the grace of the Almighty, I completed my classes at Bruni School. Hooray! Unbelievable, but I made the honor roll a few times. I still don't know how. For both Dad and Mom, it was so significant and important to see our grades – or as we called it the 'report card' at the end of the school year. All of us, myself and my brothers and sisters, would gladly show our school grades to our parents on the last day of school.

After Bruni Elementary School I would attend Katherine Tarver School for the 6th grade. My journey would continue. Eventually my desire to learn would increase. This was the journey – *mi caminata en mi vida y mis estudios*. All of this eventually would lead me to a higher learning, military service, marriage, college, and then my admission to the Diaconate program.

1937 – Myself, my sister María Elena, and my brother Jesse.

Chapter 4 – Laxatives and the Eye of the Deer
(El Ojo de Venado)

S ome call it a grocery store, a neighborhood store, or a Mom and Pop store. Bear in mind that during this period of time there were hardly any supermarkets around. In Spanish, a grocery store was a *tendajo* or a *tienda de abarrotes*. The counter, or the *mostrador* of Dad's store formed a long semicircle which I thought was very ample and with plenty of space to shop. In the center of the store was a huge red Coca Cola icebox or chest filled with ice and all kinds of cold drinks. It was about 2½ by 5 feet and about 3 feet high. And what kind of sodas were in the big ice chest? There was Coke, Grapette, Nehi, Hippo Size, RC Cola, and many others. Two double doors formed the entrance to the store. On the floor were 25- to 100-pound sacks of flour, *salvado* (bran), purina, sugar, corn, and salt. Can you imagine; you could buy five or ten cents worth of any of the items mentioned above. Incredible!

The big Coca Cola ice chest reminds me of another incident. About every three weeks a man by the name of Gil – we called him Mr. Gil – would come to the store to see what items or supplies Dad needed. Mr. Gil worked for a grocery wholesaler in town. As he walked in the store, sometimes dressed in white shirt and tie, he would grab a coke from the ice chest and gulp it down fast. Being around nine years old then, I often wondered if Mr. Gil ever paid Dad for the nickel Coke. Perhaps this was the first time in my life that I thought of what I wanted to do when I get older. Of course, I wanted to be like Mr. Gil and drink free Cokes and wear a white shirt and write down grocery orders. That looked very promising to me. Later in my life I wanted to be a cartoonist, a teacher or a writer of country ballads. The good Lord had other things in mind. Like the old adage goes: "Man proposes but God disposes." "*El hombre propone y Dios dispone.*" Now, back to the grocery store.

Most of the 100-pound flour sacks came in bright colors. Some were designed with dots, flags, trees, or rainbows. The fabric or cloth of these 100-pound sacks were to be my future underwear or shorts. On an old Singer pedal sewing machine, my mother who was a good seamstress or *costurera* designed my shorts or *calzónes*. The underwear turned out to be sturdy and artistic . . . so, move over Hanes, Jockey, and Fruit of the Loom. Let me assure all my readers that not once have I divulged information to anyone regarding my *chónes*.

On the floor around the counter were baskets with onions, tomatoes, peaches, oranges, and lemons. Behind the counter were canned goods, cookie boxes, soaps, dry goods, and tobacco and cigarettes. The most sold cigarettes of the time were the big three: Lucky Strike, Chesterfield, and Camel. On the roll-your-own tobacco, the favorites were Bugler and Bull Durham. On top of the counter was a big tray of *pan dulce* (sweet bread) and a hand-operated coffee grinder. You could purchase half-a-pound or a pound of coffee and grind it yourself. I remember the nice aroma when the coffee grinder was in operation. On the center of the counter was the cash register. On the far end of the counter of the store was the medicine section.

There was quite a selection of potions, pills, tablets, and a choice of medicinal herbs. First was the popular Dr. J. H. McLean's Volcanic Oil, generally known as *volcánico*. People used this oil for minor muscular aches and pains, for stiffness and soreness of muscles. There were the Bayer Aspirin, Milk of Magnesia, Castoria, Baby Percy, Mentholatum, and Vicks. However the humdinger and champion of all laxatives was the *Purga del Diablito*, or the "Laxative of the Little Devil." This 7-ounce bottle of clear, crystalline liquid was really the fire and brimstone of laxatives, guaranteed to clean your body throughout. Some would say that it was guaranteed not only to cleanse you but to sanctify you and give you the runs as well. As for me, the run was about 45 feet to the privy, which I could make in about 5 seconds . . . depending.

Behind the counter was a controversial item that most people have forgotten about, and for some, they would rather not talk about it. I am referring to the deer's eye or *el ojo de venado*. The deer's eye was a marble-size ornament or bead worn by a baby on a string around his wrist. The color of this bead was light brown with a black dot in the center. My memory tells me it was sold for about ten cents. Now, may I ask why on earth should a baby had to wear this witchy or sorcerous piece of string around his wrist? Some people were offended and they called it *brujería* or witchcraft. Still many believed it was *el mal de ojo* or the evil eye.

Just what is *el mal de ojo*? Mexicans and many Hispanics in the United States say this is an ailment or disorder caused by a spell from a person who looks at someone with a strong admiration. If they do not touch that person, it is believed that person could get sick with chills or fever. This applies for the most part to babies; if you look at a pretty baby and you like him or her very much, the baby should definitely be touched by the person admiring him or her. If you abstain from doing this, the child will get sick. It is called *le hiciéron ojo* or 'the evil eye got him.' Thus, *el ojo de venado* or the deer's eye. Believe it or not, if the child is wearing the deer's eye around the wrist, he will always be protected from the evil eye. Baloney!

Looking back and listening to the old-timers in Dad's store, I could sense that there was a strong belief and credence on the power of our own eyes. According to them, the eye is a magnetic force jam-packed with electricity. In view of this, you must touch that pretty child or else he is going to get sick. Do you believe this? Some would say, "What if the baby is ugly?" Is there then a need to touch the baby? Let me say here that God never makes anything ugly. All of God's creation is pretty and lovely. We are the ones who dirty and pollute this planet. Almighty God has created beauty and He has shared this beauty with mankind. He even fashioned us and made us after the design of His own body, by making us in His own image. God our creator liked everything He designed. *"God looked at everything He had made, and He found it very good."* (Genesis 1: 31)

In my third year of studies at the seminary, we had a lesson on traditions and beliefs among Mexican-Americans. The subjects covered were many. Some included bad luck, the evil eye, the *curanderos*, (healers) *sustos*, (fears) and *promesas* (promises). Naturally, this lesson was much different and distinct from the normal courses in our diaconate curriculum, which included theology, scripture, homiletics, Christology, canon law, and others. About seven deacon candidates in my class were not too happy with the lesson on the evil eye. One of the students complained to the professor as to why the need for the stupid lesson. The professor told us: "It doesn't matter if you believe or don't believe, the contents of this lesson must be taught so you can have some knowledge on the subject covered."

Many of the cultures around the world still believe in the evil eye. This belief is not only prevalent in South America, Mexico, and Third World countries but also in nations like England, Poland, France, Ireland, and Spain. Some believers are certain that the evil eye is able to cause injury or bad luck for the person at whom it is directed. So it is only to be expected that many cultures have protective measures against the evil eye; thus, *el ojo de venado*. In many Mediterranean and Asian cultures, charms, decorations, and necklaces showing the "eye" are used for protection but these charms are also popular among tourists.

In South Texas, persons affected by the evil eye can be cured through a special ceremony or ritual. This task is normally performed by a *curandero* or a knowledgeable adult. The sign of the cross is made over a raw egg and prayers follow as the *curandero* rubs the body of the sick person with the egg. Later this egg is cracked and put in a plate and left overnight under the bed of the victim. Next morning the condition of the egg will dictate if the victim was affected by *el mal de ojo*, the evil eye. If the egg appears to be cooked (make mine over easy), then this will show the healing is working. Hogwash!

In my many years living in San Antonio, I have met Hispanic and Anglo people that still believe in this superstition. At the present time this wishy-washy belief is not confined only to the illiterate, the ignoramus, the rancheros, or the border people. My dear readers, how sad it is that belief in this hocus-pocus of the "evil eye" is still alive and well in South Texas.

Chapter 5 – Katherine Tarver School
and the Río Grande

For the sixth grade, I attended the Katherine Tarver School, located in the central part of Laredo, just in front of the historic San Agustín Plaza. The distance to this school from my house was much farther than it was to Bruni School. Believe it or not, from now on Dad would not have to follow me to school with a belt. There would be times when I would have to ride the bus to downtown Laredo. However, most of the time I would walk with some of my friends . . . as we used to say then: "*andabamos a pata*" – on foot. San Agustín Plaza was the core and the center of interest for early Laredo. Katherine Tarver School was just a few blocks from the International Bridge.

Also, Tarver was just walking distance to the museum of the Republic of the Río Grande. (More on that later.) Across from the east side of the plaza is also the old but beautiful San Agustín church. In the year 2000, the Diocese of Laredo was established. San Agustín Church was confirmed as the Cathedral for the Diocese by Pope John Paul II. There is a marker across San Agustín Church that designates the original founding of Laredo in 1755 by Don Tomas Sanchez.

Laredo High School was founded in 1916, and later called the Katherine Tarver School. The original site is now taken by a La Posada Hotel, one of the top hotels in Laredo. In 1937, Laredo High School was moved to San Bernardo Avenue and renamed Martin High School. About a block south of Tarver School, and down a small precipice is the famous Río Grande River. I remember that as you descended to the river level there was brush, cactus, and bamboo plants. Many times we went to the riverbank to eat our lunch; tacos, hamburgers, chips, sandwiches, et cetera. How can I forget that the lunch hour by the river was also used for something else? There were days when we would have "friendly" rock fights with the kids across the river in Mexico. They would call us *póchos* or *gringos,* and of course we had some choice names for them also.

By all means, not all of it was rock fights and hostility. Once in a while we had our peace treaties and our *esprit de corps.* We would invite the Mexican kids to wade across and share our tacos and sandwiches. Sometimes two or three kids would cross and joined us in our river cuisine. As may be expected, it didn't last long. Peace treaties were meant to be broken and soon the rocks would start flying again. We were quite accurate in the art of rock throwing as we could easily hurl a normal rock across the Río Grande. We would also use another rock-throwing instrument; the homemade wooden slingshot, or as we called it, the *nigasúra.* In Mexico they call this an *ulera.* The Mexican kids were to some extent very accurate with another version of the sling called *la honda.* In scripture this was King David's favorite weapon. Enough on the friendly battles on the Río Grande. How about my studies at Katherine Tarver School?

It was the 6th grade, and more and more I was enjoying the classes in history and English. Also, at this time I was becoming interested in cartooning, lettering, and soon oil painting. My favorite teacher at Tarver was Mrs. Ayala, who was well versed in and dedicated to the study of history. At this time I would recall that Dad, even with his limited education, was very devoted to the study of geography. The Second World War was coming to an end. Dad would cut out and study the maps from the newspaper showing the final offensives of the Allied forces in Europe. From the maps he would show me the battles and tactics on the European front.

One subject in particular that I disliked at Tarver was reading. Every day the students would take turns and stand in front of the class and read for about five minutes. If it was my turn to read the following day, I would find a way to skip the reading class. The point was that I just couldn't stand in front of the class to read. This is plain unbelievable, even unthinkable! Why was it that in my speech classes at San Antonio College, I forgot all the fears from Tarver? Why? In my deacon formation classes at the seminary, there was a full year of homiletic studies for each candidate. We had to prepare and deliver homilies and sermons for every Sunday in the church liturgical calendar. After ordination, I preached hundreds of bilingual homilies in my parish, plus the talks and sermons for weddings, baptisms, and graveside services. In addition, I taught English and Spanish Bible classes in my parish for more than ten years. Later after ordination I was selected by Father Jack O'Donoghue, Director of Deacons, to assist in teaching homiletics to the new deacon candidates. What happened to those reading fears at Tarver School? The good Lord sure works in mysterious ways.

There was another fight, my second one while attending Tarver School – again, just a shoving match. (Shame, shame, Deacon Díaz!) Across the street from the school and almost in the center of San Agustín Plaza was the site for my second squabble. It was the general agreement or consensus of the odds makers that I handily won this fight. My record now was one lost at Bruni and one won at Tarver. These were my only two and my last scuffles in the Laredo schools. The next one, the big one, would occur in Korea about eight years later. After my Navy boot camp. I was assigned to my first aircraft carrier . . . the escort carrier *USS Badoeng Strait* CVE-116, with home port in Pearl Harbor, Hawaii. On the 25th of June 1950, North Korean communist forces invaded South Korea. A few days later President Harry S Truman ordered U.S. Army and Naval forces to defend South

Korea. Promptly, my ship joined Task Force 77 of the Seventh Fleet in attacks against the communist aggressors in North Korea. But I am getting ahead of myself.

My next school was L. J. Christen Junior High, where I would attend the 7th and 8th grades. The Katherine Tarver memories are still with me, as are the lunch hours by the Río Grande, the friendly rock fights, the mid-plaza friendly squabble, and my reading class fears. Again, these lessons would serve and eventually would be of great benefit in my journey.

Chapter 6 – Once Again – The Río Grande
El Río Bravo del Norte

Southwest of San Antonio – 145 miles to be exact – is the old and historic town of Laredo, Texas. For more than one hundred years this town has been known as "The Gateway to Mexico." Many stories, yarns, and poetry have been written about this growing metropolis. Movies have been filmed there and not too long ago a television series was showing the country a story about early Laredo. The city is located in the south-central part of Webb County and forms the entrance corridor to the Río Grande Valley. As capital of the Republic of the Río Grande, Laredo can boast of having been under seven flags instead of the traditional six. The Republic of the Río Grande existed from 1839 to late 1840, after disgruntled settlers in northern Mexico and the section of Texas south of the Nueces River rebelled against Mexico. Located near the International Bridge and just across San Agustín Plaza is the adobe building which served as capital of the Republic of the Río Grande.

Separating Laredo, Texas, and Nuevo Laredo, Mexico, is the legendary Río Grande River. This great river begins in the Rockies of southwestern Colorado, and empties into the Gulf of Mexico, thus forming an international boundary between two countries. The Río Grande has been called mighty by adventurers, beautiful by artists, romantic by lovers, and a menace by the Border Patrol. It has been labeled a fisherman's paradise and also a source of life for South Texas farmers.

To me, the Río Grande is enchanting, cruel, and bewildering. Believe it or not, the Río Grande is the twentieth longest river in the world. This is length, not width, because this river at times can be a mile wide and a foot deep and the only river in the world navigable by pedestrians. Laredoans say that this river gets so dry that sometimes birds build their nests right on the banks. This river, as I mentioned before, is a fisherman's paradise. Did you know that some catfish have been in the Río Grande for five years and still don't know how to swim? Yes my friends, this river gets so dry in August that they have to irrigate it . . . and one year it was so dry they were spraying the catfish for ticks.

A fisherman once related to me that fishing was so bad in the Río Grande that even the biggest liars didn't catch nothing. Wow! Most everyone that has fished in this river knows that the fish are relatively small in size. As a matter of fact the biggest fish ever caught in the Río Grande was only eleven inches. Of course, down here we measure them between the eyes. However, for those fishermen interested in figures and statistics, try this one for size: in 1951, an alligator gar was caught in the waters of the Río Grande. This monster fish weighed 279 pounds and measured seven feet and nine inches. This is a Texas record for gars. (See *The World Book Encyclopedia Volume VI*) And this ain't no bull.

A few miles downstream from the International Bridge was a scenic bend of the river known as *Piedra China* or Chinese Rock. I don't know if they still call it that, or even if it's still there. There were some big rocks on the edge of the river and also a small cliff. As youngsters, we would dive into the river from this cliff. To be truthful, this was the "old swimming hole." Many times the *Piedra China* area was where we played hooky or *hacer la perra*. (Shame, shame, Deacon Díaz!) *Piedra China* was not only a secluded area, but it was a pretty sight with its well-arranged rock formations.

One time my older brother Jesse, invited me to go fishing. Keep in mind that I wasn't much of a fisherman, and to be truthful, I don't like fishing.

I asked my brother, "Who in his right senses would spend half a day sitting down, waiting and waiting for a stupid fish?" He told me, "Who in his right senses would spend half a day in a cow pasture hitting a dumb little golf ball?" I rest my case. Then my brother throws a long line attached with many hooks into the river – and then we waited and waited. Later he bawled me out because I was talking. "The fish don't bite if you are talking!" he said. That did it! I'm still playing golf.

Early Spanish explorers named this river, the *Río Grande* which means 'big river.' Mexicans call the river *El Río Bravo del Norte* which means 'the bold river of the North.' As mentioned before this river is cruel, but is nevertheless enchanting. The Río Grande forms part of my childhood memories in Laredo. There is a *dicho* or saying that I used to hear from old ranchers and from some of the clients that patronized my Dad's store. They used to say that anyone who tasted the waters of the Río Grande, his steps will bring him back.

Chapter 7 – *Mi Tía Rosa* – My Aunt Rosa

"Hands that help are better than lips that pray." – Robert Ingersoll

You can get into a few arguments and quarrels with the above saying. I have always believed in prayer, but I also believe in hard work. My Tía Rosa was another in the family who trusted and deeply believed in the work ethic. Aunt Rosa, my mother's sister, was unmarried and lived in a big house with my grandmother not too far from us. After my grandma's death she moved in with us. My aunt was a beautiful lady, but at the same time she was strict and respectable. There were times when she was so tough on us that one of my sisters said she was actually our stepmother. Aunt Rosa wanted us to help around the house and not be lazy. I recall so well one of her favorite sayings: *"Gente parada, no gana nada."* "People standing around don't gain nothing."

Aunt Rosa helped my mom with the house chores, washing, ironing, and at times she helped Dad in the grocery store. Time and time again she would warn and caution us to take good care of our mother. For my part I was getting tired of the same old litany, "Take care of your mother." That is good advice, of course it is, but it got so repetitious. She would also add, "If you don't take good care of your mother, when she dies you are going to be sent to an orphanage. There, the nuns will spank you and discipline you for not taking care of your mom!" Holy cow! That couldn't be true.

So what does an ambitious, curious, and fascinated twelve-year-old do in this case? Well, I decided to conduct a complete investigation, a fact-finding mission. A young Sherlock Holmes departed on an undercover assignment to investigate the orphanage.

At this moment I don't recall if the orphanage was located on Market Street or Corpus Christi Street, but I do remember that it was in the Heights area. Upon arriving at the orphanage, I performed my observation from across the street. I remember the wrought iron fence and gate. High above the gate in big iron letters were the words: "God Shall Provide." On the grounds of the orphanage I saw young boys and girls, but at no time did I see any punishment being imposed by the wicked nuns. Perhaps I expected to see the orphans in leg iron chains, breaking rocks, being spanked, and tortured. There was no further investigation of this matter – but we still respected my Tía Rosa. All my sisters and brothers loved her. She was tough but fair and she meant well. On one occasion, after I was already married and living in San Antonio, I sent a Mother's Day card to my mother and one to Aunt Rosa also. I wrote on her card that she was like another mom to me, and how well her advice and counsel had paid off for me. The next time I was visiting in Laredo, my dear Aunt Rosa grabbed me, hugged me, and let out a good cry. In tears, she told me I was the first one who had ever said that. I couldn't stop her crying; she was so thankful. God bless her!

On the 2nd day of November, All Souls' Day, Aunt Rosa would take me on the bus to the cemetery. There she would buy flowers and take them to the gravesite of my grandfather. This day, also known as *"El día de los muertos,"* or "the day of the dead," is celebrated in Mexico, the United States, and in many countries around the world. Many of the traditions or customs for this day are mixed with Catholic observances. It is the custom, especially in South Texas, for people to visit the cemeteries where their loved ones are buried and decorate their graves with *"ofrendas"* or offerings. As I walked the cemetery grounds with my aunt I could already observe many of the things going on. First of all, it was crowded, noisy, and festive. Even as a young boy of twelve I understood that this was supposed to be a solemn and religious day to honor your dead relatives and friends. But it wasn't!

Don't get me wrong because I am sure that many people went to pray, to cry, and to pay respects to their dead. But there was something else. Outside the gates of the cemetery there were flower stands, restaurants, music, and noise. Inside was about the same. Amid all the people mourning by the burial grounds of their relatives or friends, there was also a business atmosphere around. It was there! All types of people were selling and peddling goods, merchandise, and food. For example, you could buy flowers, religious cards, statues, and of course there were different types of food: tacos, hamburgers, tostadas, cookies, and all kinds of drinks. My favorites were the *raspas* (snow cones) and sugar cane.

There were photographers who were taking pictures of people by the tombstones of their faithful departed – for a price, of course. Singers came along to serenade you and the deceased – also for a price. Someone dressed in alb and stole – who knows if they were priests or not – would offer a prayer for the deceased . . . and for a price. It was the stock exchange at its best. But here was my favorite venture; I liked it and I told my aunt about it. There was a man going to each gravesite with a small box of paint brushes and two colors of paint – silver and gold. For a price he would touch up the names on the gravestone. Being an amateur artist, this looked very easy for me, and for 50 cents a job this was quite a deal – it was a bargain. In view of all of this, the cemetery appeared to me like a money-making business arena. I am sure that no cemetery allows this now. Doesn't this remind you of Jesus driving the money changers out of the temple? *"My house shall be a house of prayer, but you are making it a den of thieves."* (Matthew 21: 12-13)

Even in November, the weather was sometimes very hot for the *"Día de los muertos."* Thank, Tía Rosa, for taking me along to the cemetery. Really, I enjoyed the *raspas* and the sweet sugar cane.

Chapter 8 – My Grandmother Gabriela

"A mother becomes a true grandmother the day she stops noticing the terrible things her children do because she is so enchanted with the wonderful things her grandchildren do."
– Lois Wyse

A wild guess is that my grandmother was not much enchanted with the wonderful things I did. Why? Because there were not many enchanted things I did. It is true, however, that in the eyes, heart, and mind of a grandma there is nothing sweeter than her grandchildren, enchanted or not. I loved my grandma as she was always there for me. She was the spoiler. In the cold winter days she spoiled me and warmed me with hot chocolate and *pan dulce*, and it was cold lemonade and *raspa* in the hot summer days. My grandma was to me God's most precious work of art. Oh yes, grandmas humor you, oblige you, cater to you, pamper you, and they love you. Anything else?

As a child I noticed that all grandmothers looked old. Nowadays that is not true. Grandmas look younger. Could it be Maybelline, Helena Rubenstein, and Max Factor? No, I am just kidding. In my ministry as a deacon I baptized many babies with teenage mothers. Sometimes the baby's grandma was present as a *madrina* (godmother) and many times I mistook her for the mother. But what really is a grandmother? One unknown poet said that, "A grandmother is one with silver on her hair and gold in her heart."

My Grandma Gabriela had an old but beautiful parrot. She called him *Lorito* which means 'little parrot.' Patience is the mother of all virtues; needless to say, Grandma had plenty of patience. I witnessed much of that as she taught and talked to her *Lorito*. In the backyard of her house there was a huge pirul tree. This tree is recognized by its floppy leaves and clusters of pinkish red berries. Sometimes it is called a Peruvian or California peppercorn tree. As children we were told that the berries were poisonous. Lorito the parrot would climb to the highest point of the pirul tree. Repeatedly my grandma would call the parrot to get down. After so much begging, down comes the pampered brat.

Grandma Gabriela patiently taught Lorito to say the first words of the Lord's Prayer. *"Padre Nuestro que estás en el Cielo"* – "Our Father who art in Heaven." Lorito would repeat the first six words of the Lord's Prayer. Parrots repeat themselves so much. So he would repeat the words over and over again. One day my neighbor friend Eduardo (Wayo) and I were teaching Lorito something that wasn't nice. Let's say they were not good words like *cabron* and *chingado* plus a few other Irish words. Soon enough he was saying those nasty words. I don't suppose Grandma never found out who were the culprits, but I bet she had a good idea. (Shame, shame, Deacon Díaz!)

Grandmothers love their grandchildren, and vice versa, grandchildren love their grandmas. My two daughters always wanted to visit their Grandma Julia and Grandma Panchita in Laredo. Many times my mother would ask my wife and me to leave our two daughters with her for a week or two. "They are my two lovely angels; I love them so much!" my mother used to say. As I reflect on my two girls at the age of about five or six years old, one incident comes to mind. During the hot months I would get after them to stay out of the sun as they played in the backyard. And during the rainy days they liked to play in the mud. Despite all this caution and advice about the mud, I never understood why they wanted to go see their grandmas in Laredo. For sure! Their grandmas were enjoying and playing with their granddaughters in the mud – making mud pies. Can you beat that? Someone once said that as long there are godly grandmothers there will always be love in this world. I agree with that.

Thank you, Grandmas, for loving your grandchildren. Presently, this world needs more love. I'll close with an Italian proverb that says: "If nothing is going well, call your grandmother."

10th Grade, Martin High School, Laredo, Texas.

Chapter 9 – L. J. Christen Middle School and Martin High School

How about that! *"Ave María Purisima."* I am now in middle school. Once again I can walk home for a good hot lunch instead of the familiar cold taco/sandwich midday meal that I was eating on the benches of San Agustín Plaza and on the banks of the Río Grande. L. J. Christen School is located on Park Street and Santa María Avenue and adjoins Martin High School. Many of my early school friends who were with me at Bruni were still around. For the first time I would now be able to attend gym classes. Also available were the sports activities I could try out for, like baseball, football, track, and soccer. Of course my favorites were baseball and track.

My interest in the subjects of English and history was expanding. For the most part I enjoyed Texas and U.S. history. Later in life I would be attracted and fascinated with church and world history. One of my favorite teachers at Christen was Mrs. Lindsey, who was well qualified in teaching mathematics but she was also helpful with the academic progress of all students.

Here is a little episode about the school principal and the Jolly Roger. One cold morning two other kids and I were standing by the entrance of Christen School. Staring and astonished, we were looking at the flag of the crossed bones and skull which someone had raised up on the flagpole. This flag is known as the Jolly Roger. It was still early, so the janitor had not raised the U.S. colors yet. The school principal, who was always early, stopped to look at the forbidden flag. He cracked a smile, but at the same time he looked angry and enraged.

For all of you landlubbers and pollywogs who are not familiar with this flag, let me point out that the Jolly Roger is an offensive signal and warning for war. In the old days of sailing, the Jolly Roger flag was flown to identify the ship's crew as pirates, looters, and thieves. Many countries have outlawed the flying of the Jolly Roger from their boats and ships. Incidentally, this information comes from an old salt, sea dog, and shellback; and who might that be? Thus, the principal was angry and he asked us if we knew who raised that banner up the flagpole. We didn't know, nobody knew and until now it remains a mystery of the grand ol' Jolly Roger bravely flying on the campus of Christen Middle School.

As I reflect on my two years in the 7th and 8th grade at Christen School, the first thing that comes to mind was how swiftly time went by. I believe that my two years of study at Christen were a good introduction, preparing me not only for Martin High School but to drill me for the coming projects in my future.

I began classes at Martin High School in September of 1945. The initiation committee was ready for us freshman. By tradition, the "fish" were to be given the works. Some of us were assembled, and others were individually marked with lipstick, our hair was roughly cut, *trasquilados* we called it then, and some of us had to carry posters saying: "The fish of Martin High." Even the girls received this complimentary initiation from the upper grades. The question here is, were all these initiation rituals and ceremonies legal? School officials insisted that such harassment was not right and it should not be carried out. However, the practice continued. Some students admitted that there were times when these initiations got out of hand. Obviously, this was rather minor in comparison to the initiation that new seafarers receive when you cross the equator, the domain of *Neptunus Rex* or King Neptune. In Navy tradition you are initiated as a pollywog and then promoted to a shellback.

At this time there were military veterans registering for high school. These were our heroes who served in the Army and Navy during World War II. Because of the war, their studies were interrupted and they went gallantly to foreign lands to fight for our country. Never once did I see one of our war veterans initiated with the "fish" ritual as we were. I wonder why?

In my freshman year at Martin, it was the normal subjects that were assigned to me . . . English, math, Spanish, history, and science. However, there was a new subject on the agenda. It was ROTC or military training. If you were not in sports, or the band, you had to enroll in military training. I told Dad about my new subject. He liked it and reminded me: *"Un día lo vas a necesitar."* "One day you will need this." How right he was!

On my third year of ROTC and for the first time in my life, I got to fire the old M1 Garand 30-caliber rifle in the underground range. In a few more years I would get additional training with the Navy on this rifle. Like we used to say, the M1 had quite a kick. *"Tenía buena patada."* Let me add that the M1 kick was a bit lighter than the ancient 12-gauge double-barrel shotgun that Dad owned. Eventually, I got to fire that old shotgun a few times, and the kick was brutal. I was only 15 years old.

As much as I loved sports, particularly baseball, why then did I leave sports out of my high school schedule? This is important and I have written about this in a later chapter. Of the school subjects mentioned above, I actually enjoyed them all, but I liked history and English best – and later, a new subject, mechanical drawing. Around this time in school my memories flashed back to the early days at Bruni. Back then I had said that school and church were not my piece of cake. So what happened? More is coming on that – stay tuned.

It seemed that the majority of my teachers at Martin High were excellent. Many were fully dedicated to their teaching profession. Certain zealous teachers that come to mind are English teacher Mrs. Andrews; Mrs. Cox, History; Miss Uribe, typing and accounting; the flamboyant English teacher, Miss Christillies, and of course, a friend of all, Mr. Shoenberg, who taught mechanical drawing.

One of my special teachers and mentors was Captain August Hein, professor of military science and tactics, who had fought under General Patton in World War II. Capt. Hein was tough as nails, but he was a fair man. He was the only person I saw who would put out his cigarette on the palm of his left hand. One afternoon I recall, he was looking at our company that was marching in the hot sun. Unexpectedly, he stopped the company and told us in a loud voice: "The way you are marching, you look like a bunch of bums looking for nickels on the ground. You better improve and shape up, because I have a feeling that very shortly I will see you guys in Egypt or Korea." That was Capt. Hein's early prediction for the next war. Most of us had never heard of Korea, but he was right. It happened! He told us this in the spring of 1948. The Korean War started in 1950.

My social life at Martin was dull and aimless. Never did I attend a junior-senior prom or any other social function. Neither was I a member of a school club or activity. The only exception was that in my last two years at Martin I was doing some art work and lettering for the school yearbook, *La Pitahaya*. For most of the four years in high school, I worked after school and weekends. But let me go back a bit to the subject of social life at Martin High; I do remember some of the guys talking about their girlfriends and their dates.

A favorite question was: "During the weekend, what restaurant did you take your girlfriend to for dinner?" For the major part, the answer was either the Southland Cafe or the Plaza Hotel, and usually not true, since at that time they were the two most expensive restaurants in downtown Laredo. The reply from the other person was: "Who are you trying to impress, you probably took her to *Los Baños*!"

What were *Los Baños*? On the first plaza across the river in Nuevo Laredo, Mexico, there was a man with two *baños*, or washtubs filled with *elotes* – that is corn on the cob. That was the fancy *Los Baños* restaurant, where the meal was consumed standing on your two feet. So the guys would take their dates to eat corn on the cob at *Los Baños*. According to many who ate there, the corn was delicious. There was butter and salt available and the corn was warm and tasty. But there is more to the story. When someone would say: "Did you notice that the corn tasted a bit spicy? You know why? They used the tub to bathe their children the night before!"

Another place where the guys were accused and blamed for taking their dates for lunch was the popular *El Chore* restaurant on San Bernardo Street. Would you believe five-cent hamburgers with lettuce, onion, and tomatoes? Yes, that's absolutely correct. Nickel hamburgers and nickel cokes and no sale tax. Where were you, McDonald's?

There were times when the whole ROTC Battalion would march in downtown Laredo on Friday afternoon. This was more like a pep rally for the coming football game that evening. We would also march on the annual Washington's Birthday Celebration parade. This was a well-viewed spectacle, in the years before television, as thousands of people lined the streets of Laredo to see the great international parade.

Finally, graduation day arrived. That evening, the mighty class of 1949 gathered in the school gymnasium and we wore our caps and gowns for the first and the last time. Best wishes and congratulations were offered among the students and some of the teachers that were also present. From the gym we marched in procession to Shirley Stadium for the ceremony, as we listened to the beautiful and inspiring music of "Pomp and Circumstance." No doubt about it, we were on cloud nine. It was a great event in my life. My Mom and Dad were present. I was somewhat startled to see Dad, as he seldom, if ever attended such events. Finally, after the customary and lengthy speeches, the diplomas were presented to us. We were now graduates of the mighty Martin High School, class of '49. After the graduation formalities there was so much joy and happiness, but it was also a sentimental and tear-jerking time for many students. I could hear it from some students: "I made it!" "*Gracias a Dios*," (thank God) and others would say: "*Ya era tiempo,*" or, "It was about time." Some teachers came to us in tears to wish us well. I couldn't help thinking were they putting on an act or were they pretending? Perhaps they were crying joyfully and happily because they would not see our ugly faces again. (Shame, shame, Deacon Díaz!)

Graduation was a wake-up call for me. In my mind I thought of those dreadful days when I disliked any kind of schooling. Now, as a high school graduate, I had an incentive and a push to go on with my education. I was realizing just how important my education was. How blessed I was to have behind me the support and the prayers of a good mother and father. Furthermore, I was so sure that my Creator God would protect me and guide me in my journey. *"He guides me in right paths for his name's sake. Even though I walk in the dark valley I fear no evil; for YOU are at my side."* (Psalm 23)

"For when the one Great Scorer comes to mark against your name, He writes not that you won or lost, but how you played the game." – Grantland Rice

These words are inscribed in a marker at the entrance to Shirley Stadium, Martin High School, Laredo, Texas.

Chapter 10 - Sports

"Show me a good and gracious loser and I'll show you a failure." – Knute Rockne

Just north from my childhood residence in Laredo was an empty block of land with plenty of brush, weeds, and cactus. This was the barrio Yankee Stadium and the birthplace of my baseball legacy. It was originally named San Luis Field and presently it is Al King Field. At the time there was no Little League baseball, or other sports organizations for the youth. On Saturdays of the summer months, the San Luis baseball team gathered together to clean the brush, cut some cactus, and get the field ready for play. We had a strong team, as some of the players included three of the Luna brothers, a legendary baseball family. There was two of the Guevara family boys, myself, and other kids from the neighborhood. What we had for baseball equipment was nothing to brag about. We had crooked old bats, ugly baseballs, and even some of our gloves were homemade. But good heavens, what we lacked in equipment we made it up with our scrappy and aggressive baseball squad.

We played other neighborhood teams and some came from distant barrios in Laredo to San Luis field, just to get beat. Sometimes we had small crowds watching us as they stood in the street and endured the scorching Laredo sun to cheer for their team. Later, the Luna brothers and I started playing for the Rotarian baseball team of the newly-formed American Legion league. God bless the American Legion, which ranks as the oldest veterans organization in the United States. This patriotic group not only seeks to advance the interests of veterans, but also was very active in the education and sports for the youth. Our team sponsor was the Rotarian Club of Laredo. Our coach was Brother William Vessels of the Marist Brothers religious congregation, who was also a teacher at Saint Joseph's Academy. Some of the San Luis players were members of the Rotarian baseball team of the newly-formed American Legion league.

The American Legion was a well-organized league stressing fair play and sportsmanship in the game of baseball. Other teams in the league were sponsored by the local organizations and companies: LULAC, Elks, Dr Pepper, DeMolay, and the Optimists. We had a strong team, and for the first two years in its existence the Rotarians won the American Legion championship. The old and antiquated Washington ball park was the only baseball field in Laredo. All the American Legion ball games were played there. I really believe that it is fitting and proper to recognize my Rotarian team members and champs of the American Legion league. They were: Felipe Luna and Manuel Rodriguez, catchers, Simón Luna, Gume Hernandez, pitchers, Felix García, 1st baseman, me, 2nd baseman, Pete Luna, 3rd baseman, Hector Garcia, shortstop; outfielders were Albert Dutson, Neo Guevara, Jesus Garcia, and E. Aguilar. At the end of the season an all-star team was selected to represent Laredo. At least five players from the Rotarian team made the all-star team when we beat McAllen for the district championship, and then Corpus Christi to reach the quarter-finals of the state of Texas, where we lost to the powerful Austin American Legion team in the state capital.

For two years in a row the Rotary Club of Laredo honored its baseball championship team with a magnificent luncheon at the grand and luxurious Plaza Hotel. At the time this was the most elaborate hotel in Laredo. What the heck, there were only two hotels then! District Rotarian officers were present along with some political biggies from the Independent political club (*El partido viejo*). I am quite sure that most of the barrio champion baseball players were out of place at this champion's luncheon. I know I was. It was a posh, ritzy setting. For the first time in my life, I saw in front of me two dinner plates, two forks, two spoons, knife, fancy glass, cup and saucer, and a beautiful large blue and white napkin. Wow! After all the speeches and accolades, our names were called individually to approach the podium to receive a beautiful and well-earned medal; I still have mine. Coach Brother William was also given a special award.

After my baseball days with the Rotarian club of the American Legion in Laredo I would not play any more baseball until my return from Korea, when I played with the potent Great Lakes Naval Training Center Blue Jacket team. Then I began skidding, or should I say that I began playing fast-pitch softball and slow-pitch (I call it the ladies game) at Kelly AFB. Next was the gallant and ridiculous game of golf, which I will address in a later chapter. However, baseball was my game – my piece of cake. I loved it and the memories of the game will stay with me forever.

The Laredo Boys Club was a great showplace for Laredo. It was a place for education and sports. The spacious library was a place for the kids to read, study, and do their homework. All kinds of games were available, including table tennis or ping pong, billiards, and a huge and beautiful swimming pool was accessible to all members. Then there was a gymnasium and a full basketball court. I played basketball for two years with the Boys Club team which belonged to the Laredo Teen Age league. Other teams in the league included those sponsored by the Holding Institute, Saint Joseph's Academy, Aduana from Nuevo Laredo, Saint Peters, LULAC, and Saint Augustine. Among the Boys Club players were; Poncho and Arturo Garza, Elías Prieto, Juan Ríos, Luis Ibarra, Lico Paez, Anthony Pena, Ignacio Flores, Tony Veliz, Julio Castillo and me. Our coaches were Joe Prieto and Jack Preston. Our strong Boys Club team won the Teen

Age league twice and we also played some of the high schools in the area, like Bruni, Hebbronville, and Benavides High Schools.

Another sport I participated in was table tennis or ping pong. In the annual tournament I was the city runner-up champion to my friend and later a Korean War hero, Luis Ibarra. Later, Luis and I teamed up to win the Laredo teenage doubles crown in ping pong. Also at the Boys Club, Laredo's radio station KPAB held a 30-minute live show. Boys Club members would read, tell stories, sing, or have special shows on the radio. Guess what? On one occasion I sang. Yes, and it was a country song that was made popular by the late governor of Louisiana, Jimmy Davis. The song was "Makes No Difference Now." So to my brother Chalo who loves music and was a DJ in Houston – take that. What do you say of the teenage Laredo troubadour?

1948 Rotary Team – American Legion Baseball League. I am in the front row.

Laredo Boys Club championship basketball team – I am #6.

Chapter 11 – The United States Navy

In May 1949, I graduated from Martin High School. On the 6th of June of the same year I enlisted in the U. S. Navy. Some weeks before graduation I had informed my parents about my plans to join the Navy. Immediately I could sense some sorrow or despair in my mother's face and I saw a few tears as she imparted her blessing on me. Dad also gave me his blessing but at the same time voiced some of his words of wisdom. One of them was: *"Mi hijo, obedece a tus superiores; vas a servir en el cuerpo militar mas poderoso del mundo, que Dios te bendiga."* "My son, obey your superiors, you will serve in the most powerful military force in the world. May God bless you." On the subject of obedience, the great saint and doctor of the Catholic Church, Saint Thomas Aquinas, wrote in his fabulous *Summa Theologica*: "Obedience is the virtue by which a man submits his own will to the commands of a superior. It is natural that children should obey their parents, that citizens should obey their government, that military men should obey their commanders, and that all men should obey God. Without obedience to their superiors, men can never establish in society that order which is needed if they are to obtain that share of the common good which is necessary for their own happiness. And without obedience to God, man can never attain happiness at all."

It was at the American Legion in Laredo where I took my entrance examination and the oath of enlistment for the U.S. Navy. Soon after, I was sent to the Veteran's Hospital in Houston for my medical examination. From there, I was sent by train (Pullman car) to the U.S. Naval Training Center in San Diego, California, to commence my eleven weeks of boot camp training. It was a long trip to San Diego and it gave me plenty of time to go over some of my thoughts. Why join the Navy? First, I would serve and defend my country. Secondly, this would be an ideal way to launch my career as I was being offered extensive job opportunities and some exceptional benefits, especially in education. Hopefully, I could develop myself both personally and professionally. I tried to sleep aboard a train for the first time in my life, but I was still hurting from those painful vaccinations and shots they gave me in Houston. Must I repeat, I don't like shots or inoculations?

My first night at a Navy base was tense and restless. The barracks was well-kept, and we would continue to keep it clean. This would be my home for the next eleven weeks. Early the first morning, just outside the barracks and still in our civilian clothing, fifty-eight young recruits from all parts of the United States were awaiting the arrival of our company commander. As we waited on that brisk spring morning, I noticed a huge sign in front of us. The exact words of that sign are still well-lodged in my mind. In big blue letters on a white background it read as follows: "You are now men of the United States Navy. When you are given an assignment, do it willingly, do it the right way, do it the Navy way." Deep in my mind I wondered: "What happened to God's way?"

After a short while, our company commander appeared and from a platform he was ready to greet us – and what a greeting! He was a sharp man, well-decorated and with more than sixteen years of naval service. It was a lengthy talk that he gave us and this is part of what he said: "Good morning, ladies. I am Chief Petty Officer Rigmaiden, and I will be your company commander (Company 137). Listen very careful to what I have to say. As I look at you right now, I do not ever recall seeing such a bunch of freaks and misfits. But, that is no problem because I will straighten and shipshape all of you. For the next eleven weeks I will not only be your company commander, but I will be your mother, father, counselor, director, and leader. Your soul might belong to God, but your rear end belongs to me because I will kick it whenever you get out of line. And you cannot call your Mommy either. All you Mama's chubby biscuit-eaters and sissies, I will turn you into real men. I give you my pledge that in eleven weeks of boot camp I will turn you into lean, mean, fighting machines. You belong now to the most powerful Navy in the whole world. [Exactly what my Dad had told me.] After eleven weeks of training, after I finish with you then I will rejoice when I call you a true, valiant American sailor. Any questions?"

There was a complete silence. Finally, Chief Rigmaiden told us: "First thing on the agenda today is that you are getting a good Navy regulation haircut to get rid of your bangs, pigtails, and perms." [The long-hair "hippie" generation was not here yet.] After that, you will be issued your Navy clothing and your piece. [But what is a piece? It was the M1 rifle.] Reveille tomorrow will be at 0500 hours. That's all."

Chief Rigmaiden kept his promise. He was strict and demanding and soon he knew all of us by name. In the meantime we absorbed the lessons of boot camp. We had seamanship and navigation courses. There was M1 firing on the range, drilling for one hour every day, the semaphore, medical training, and swimming. (If you did not learn how to swim, you could not go on leave after boot camp.) We had to dive from high altitudes and swim under a pool of fire. It was exciting! In all of this we made Chief Rigmaiden proud as we won a number of ribbons for our company's banner. There was rigid competition with the other companies in boot camp. Some of the first-place awards that we won were for drilling, marksmanship, and barracks cleanliness. The Chief was smiling and appreciating the effort and the awards won by Company 137.

Finally it was graduation. Boot camp was over. In the huge parade grounds all the graduating companies assembled and then marched by the reviewing stand in dress white uniform with leggings. The admiral commanding was there, along with other high-ranking brass and many other people. Surely this was a huge parade and display as the whole brigade of Navy graduate recruits marched with exactitude to the music of the "Colonel Bogey March." This march is the Academy Award-winning tune the British soldiers whistled in the movie *Bridge on the River Kwai.*

Chief Rigmaiden was a happy man. He had kept his promise. His prophecy was right. Perhaps not everyone in Company 137 was lean, but it was certain that we were a tough, mean, fighting machine. Three cheers for Chief Rigmaiden! His leadership and influence was a great impact on all of us recruits. We were so proud of him. What a man! His last words to the graduating sailors of Company 137 were the following: "Be proud of the uniform you wear, be good patriots." Which reminded me of the words General George Patton said: "Patriotism means making the other poor damned bastard die for his country before he can make you die for yours." After boot camp all of us received different assignments. Some would attend a service school, or duty at a naval base, and others would report for sea duty aboard one of the many warships of the Pacific Fleet. Who was to know that in less than a year some of these ships would be in the Korean War?

After my two-week leave in Laredo, I reported to my new assignment which was the aircraft carrier *USS Badoeng Strait,* CVE-116, with its home port at Pearl Harbor, Hawaii. This was a small class of carrier with only 24 planes aboard. Among those aircraft was the F4U Corsair, a workhorse and a gutsy fighter of WWII. How well I remember building a Corsair model airplane when I was still in high school.

In June of 1950, North Korean communist forces invaded South Korea. President Harry Truman ordered U.S. Army and Naval forces to defend South Korea. Without delay we loaded aircraft, ammo, and the squadron personnel and got underway for our new destination in the Sea of Japan. There we joined Task Force 77 of the Seventh Fleet in attacks against the communist aggressors in North Korea. In September 1950, my ship participated in the invasion of Inchon and the evacuation of Hungnam in December of the same year. The ship and its personnel were awarded three battle stars. Also we were awarded the Republic of South Korea Medal, the United Nations Medal, and the Navy Occupation Medal (with the Asia clasp). An added note here is that two of my friends were also in Task Force 77 and their ships also participated in the Inchon invasion. Diego Peña, my classmate from the class of 1949, Martin High School, was aboard the heavy cruiser *USS Rochester* (CA-124) and Raul Iruegas, parishioner from church. He was aboard the battleship *USS Iowa* (BB-61). About this time President Truman (God bless him) extended all Navy personnel on active duty an extra year, without raising your hand or signing a piece of paper – like it or not. No problem.

After fourteen months the *Badoeng Strait* reported to the Bremerton, Washington, shipyard for dry-dock. A few months later, I received orders to report to the heavy aircraft carrier *USS Antietam*, based in Alameda, California. This ship was just coming out of mothballs and in due time would also join Task Force 77 in the Sea of Japan. A note of interest here is that after her tour in Korea, the *Antietam* had the honor and distinction of being the first canted or angled deck carrier in the United States Navy. So, I went back to Korea, this time aboard a huge carrier with over 45 aircraft (all jets) ready for war. After eleven months on the *Antietam* I was eligible to apply for shore duty. I put in as my first choice for shore duty the Naval Base in Corpus Christi, the Navy establishment closest to

Laredo. My second choice was the Naval Base in New Orleans. The Navy, being exact and considerate in their assignments, gave me orders to report to the Service School Command at the Naval Base in Great Lakes, Illinois. That's the Navy for you!

On guard duty – boot camp.

Chapter 12 – Frog Legs, Japanese Beer, and the French Navy

After weeks at sea, it was Sasebo, Japan, or Pusan, South Korea, where ships of Task Force 77 of the Seventh Fleet would moor or lay anchor. These were our rest and recreation and our liberty ports. They were two bustling seaports where Navy ships of the United Nations came for repairs, maintenance, and for supplies and ordnance. There were fighting ships from Australia, New Zealand, Canada, France, England, and the United States. Forming the task force were destroyers, mine sweepers, light and heavy cruisers, aircraft carriers, and battleships.

Not too far from fleet landing was a spacious building that was known as the Kasbah. There was a fancy restaurant on the 1st floor and a bar on the 2nd floor. Of course, the bar could be also described as a pub, a gin mill, beer joint, tavern, or honky-tonk. Each Navy had their favorite name for the bar. The Kasbah's favorite foods on their menu were frog legs, hush puppies, and Japanese Asahi beer. On the other hand, the Kasbah was also known for its brawls and free-for-alls – friendly brawls of course. What do you expect when sailors from all over the world get together for a short, friendly beer? The New Zealanders would fight the Australian sailors, the Canadians against the British, and the U.S. fleet would fight anyone. Talk about naval and sea warfare; holy cow and shiver my timbers – that was a blast. Who would ever imagine? I thought we were fighting North Korea.

Back to the restaurant. Who in the world would ever fancy a young sailor from the brush country of South Texas eating and enjoying some delicious frog legs and Asahi beer 6,670 miles away from Laredo? Incredible! That was the first time I ate frog legs and I found them tasty and succulent. However, I must admit that it took me a while to decide if I was going to savor those ugly creatures with bulging eyes, a croaking voice and long black legs. I remembered those small frogs in the Laredo area that came out after a short rain. They were ugly ones that we stepped on and threw away. For some people those little frogs were actually something to be afraid of. As youngsters, we use to tell the girls: "*Tienes ojos de rana.* You have frog eyes." (Shame, shame, Deacon Díaz!)

How well I recall that in my second year at San Antonio College in our biology class each student was given a large African frog. We dissected this frog as part of the assignment. And in all amazement. I would say: "How can people eat such horrible species." I did! Many times I wondered how in heaven could I eat and digest those ugly amphibians in Sasebo, Japan. Maybe because I missed the homemade *fideo* with garbanzo and meat, corn tortillas, and refried beans of the brush country. And as I reflect back, there has been only one time that I have indulged in frog legs and hush puppies (no Asahi beer) since those days in Sasebo in the early 50's.

Enter the French Navy! One cold day after my ship had been out at sea for some time, I was at the Kasbah with my shipmate Robert Gaston from Lincoln, Nebraska. Of course, we were enjoying the customary meal . . . frog legs, hush puppies, and Asahi beer. On a table just across from ours were two young French sailors eating and conversing in Spanish. "This can't be," I said. "I'm hearing things. I just had one Asahi. They are French! Why are they talking in Spanish?" I couldn't stand it any longer, so after lunch, I introduced myself, in Spanish of course. What a shock it was for them also. They could not believe it either. One of them quickly exclaimed: "An American sailor talking in Spanish!" In about two hours of conversation, three sailors from different parts of the world, with different cultures and language, emerged as friends and shipmates. However, there was still in my mind the question as to why they were speaking Spanish? Well, they told me. Both of the French sailors were born near the Pyrenees Mountains, which forms the natural boundary between Spain and France. Both could speak Spanish and one of them was married to a Spanish girl.

Oftentimes when elements of Task Force 77 pulled into Sasebo, I got to see my new French/Spanish friends from the Pyrenees. Their ship was a destroyer-type vessel, which the French called a corvette. On one occasion they asked me if it could be possible for them to visit my ship. They had never been aboard an aircraft carrier. So I agreed; I took them aboard and went straight to my place of work, the ship's personnel office, where I introduced them to my boss, Chief Personnelman Timothy McPherson. The French sailors were astonished, I might say, to see some of the weaponry on the hangar deck of the carrier. The next day in the office, my Chief asked me: "Díaz, I didn't know you spoke French." With a smirk smile I replied, "Oh, heck yes, Chief, I speak French, English, and Spanish!" You know what? Since then and until now, I do not know a single word of French. Except *"Merci."*

It was unforgettable, the last time I saw my two French buddies. They took me up to "the hills." This area was the indigent and poverty-stricken area in Sasebo. In Navy terminology this was the "skid row" district. We took a small crowded trolley to the hills. On my way up there I was unable to forget that the area was also off-limits; that is to say, it was forbidden for U.S. Navy personnel. When we got there, I saw French sailors, Navy personnel from other countries, and a few American sailors. And as I looked around the congested area I wondered why the big deal, and why was it that French sailors would much rather go up to the hills?

I already knew! My two French amigos had already given me the candid and direct reason: money. French sailors preferred the hills because souvenirs, food, and booze were cheaper. Jittery and with some anxiety I looked around for the U.S. Navy Shore Patrol. Since this place was off limits, you could be put on report for breaking the law if you were caught up there. There was a small procession in the downtown section. I didn't know what was going on, but in a small plaza by the market place jugglers and magicians performed for the people. I thought they were very talented and well-coordinated. Also, I stopped to see some young Japanese boys who were drawing some caricatures – more along my line.

It was getting dark and time to get back to the ship. Liberty did not expire until 0600 hours the following morning. Once I got down the hill I would catch a rickshaw that would take me to the fleet landing where my ship was moored. But while waiting for the trolley they informed us: "No trolley, broke down," just like that. What do we do now? No problem. My friends told me that we would walk down the hill and it was only about 30 minutes to town. They told me that at times they would rather walk than take the trolley down the hill. Why? Save money. We started walking down hill at a fast pace as it was getting dark. I could now see the harbor lights in Sasebo.

I was wearing the dress blue uniform. They were wearing a lighter blue uniform which was the uniform of the day. As soon as we reached downtown Sasebo, we noticed red on the bottom of our pants, our socks and shoes. It was blood. Where in the world did we get that blood? Some days later we pulled out to sea. One evening I was told by one of my shipmates how that happened to him also. There was a hospital on that hill, which we passed as we walked down to the harbor. They threw all kinds of rags in a two-block square pit. As we walked downhill, my French shipmates and I were actually walking on bloody rags thrown away by the hospital. *"Madre mía, donde ando?" "Good mother, where am I?"*

After that incident of the bloody pants and shoes, it was the last time I saw my French buddies. I missed them! Through scuttlebutt – Navy gossip or hearsay – I heard that the French corvette had left our task force. We were also told that the corvette, while in another seaport, was sabotaged and part of the bow blown off. This was never confirmed.

The famous Kasbah, in Sasebo, Japan.

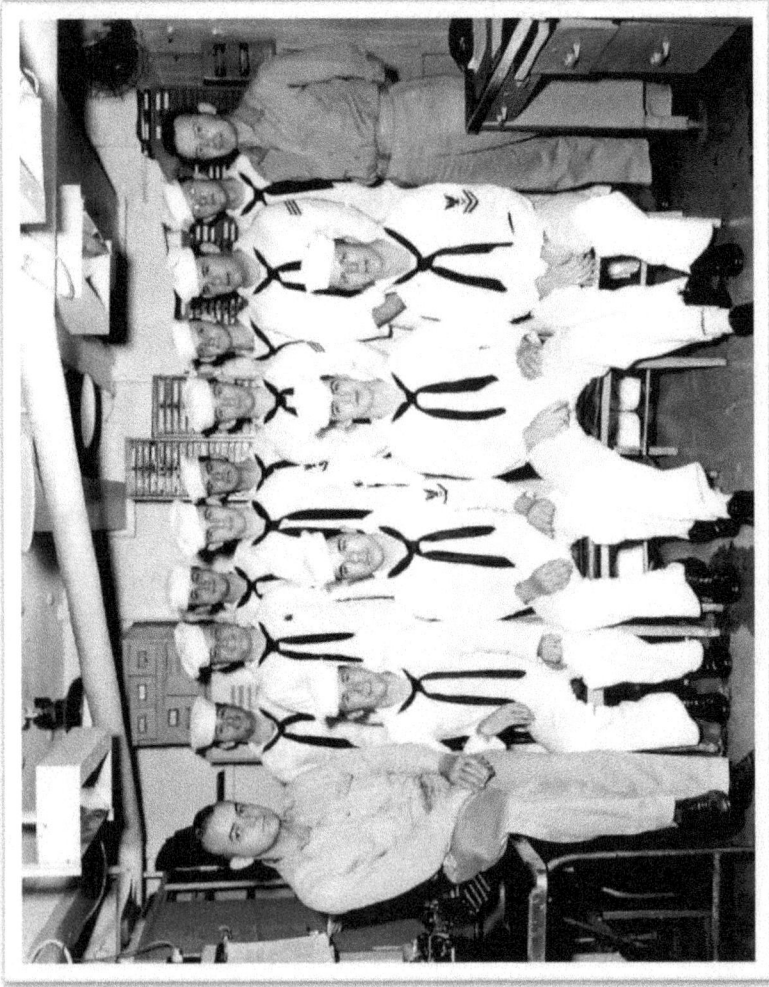

1951 - The ship's office personnel, USS Antietam (CV-36).

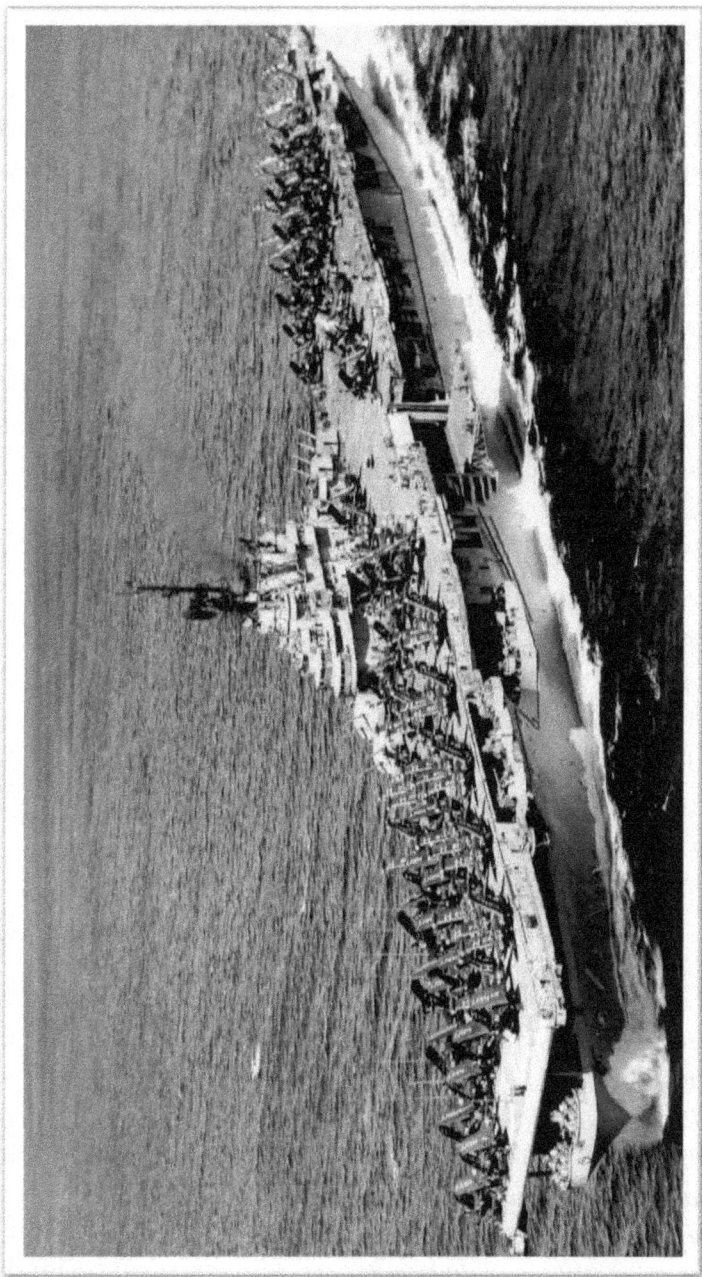

1951 – The USS Antietam, (CV-36) in Korean waters.

Chapter 13 – Shore Duty – Great Lakes, Illinois

It was a very cold night when I arrived at the central train station in Chicago. There was snow on the ground and more was expected. Carrying my Navy sea bag and a duffel, I changed trains and climbed into the Skokie railway car that would take me about 25 miles north to the Great Lakes Naval Base. Once on my way there, I had time to reflect – as I often still do – on my tour of duty aboard the two aircraft carriers. Now, there will be no more sea duty, no more battle stations, watches, general quarters, typhoons, squalls, or seasickness. Nevertheless, the tour of duty on those two warships was a deep learning experience for me. It was needed!

As I traveled on that small train car to Great Lakes, my reflections pertaining sea duty covered not only seamanship or my duties as personnel man in the ship's office but, believe it or not, my spiritual training. The sea had much to do with my early close relationship with my Creator. Unexpectedly, a beautiful poem came to mind. It was a poem about the sea that I will share with you. As a matter of fact, that is the name of the poem *The Sea*. I don't know who wrote it, but I memorized it without delay. Read it slowly as it calls attention to the beauty and the cruelty of the sea.

THE SEA

No one who has ever sailed the sea,
And answered her highest sigh,
Can banish the love of the sea from his heart,
If ever he seeks to try.
For the sea is like a woman,
Both jealous and fair and cruel as a girl can be,
And she will never part with a sailor's heart,
If he struggles and strives to be free.

Mountains and valleys and the open road, trees and a pretty sky,
Bring peace to the hearts of city tired men
Whose work is to sell or buy.
But there is never a stop in there,
For wanderers such as we,
Who danger our bodies and souls, for a kiss from the lips of the sea.

Brave we be and our term of life,
And nowhere we settle or go,
Can carry us out of the range of her call,
Wherever the high winds blow.
And whenever they tell of the guys that I knew,
Careless and brave and free,
When we would work like men and fight like men,
And love like men, the sea!

For those who have not sailed the sea let me say that it is a place where you will obtain a great deal of practical knowledge. The sea is majestic, boundless, and powerful; beautiful but yet cruel. The sea is where you work, where you meditate, and where you learn many skills. It is the rough seas that will make you or break you. On many occasions I began to realize the powerful force of the sea. *"Who has measured in his hand the waters of the sea."* (Isaiah 40: 12) God holds the seven seas on the palm of His hand. You do not need to be a rocket scientist to understand this. Simply, the prophet Isaiah is showing us the greatness, the power, and the majesty of God. I began to understand the sufficiency of God and that He has all the power and no one else – His power is unlimited.

I used to imagine just how the winds of the sea could move and shake a 58-thousand ton aircraft carrier like a piece of paper. Who is behind this great force and strength? It was scary and horrendous sometimes. At night when you tried to sleep, you could hear the heavy winds and waves pounding and crashing the side of the ship. One day as we were heading back to port, the ship was going through part of a brutal typhoon. As the ship tossed and tumbled, my friend Robert Gaston told me he was so scared that he even composed some prayers.

"*No que no chiquito!*" Robert never went to church and now he was frightened and scared-stiff, so he turned to God. Somehow the sea will make you tough and strong. Thus, the English proverb reads: "A smooth sea never makes a skillful sailor." Being on a big ship with over two thousand sailors and over 45 aircraft aboard, we rated three chaplains: a Catholic priest, a Protestant minister, and a Jewish rabbi. There were some Sundays that we could attend Catholic Mass. By the way, Mass was only 15 to 20 minutes long, depending on the battle watch conditions.

It was nearly midnight when I finally reached my destination – the U.S. Naval Training Center, Great Lakes, Illinois. This giant naval base is located between Chicago and Milwaukee, Wisconsin. At the time, Great Lakes not only consisted of a full-scale training center which had over five thousand naval recruits but it was the headquarters for the Navy Service School Command. This huge base had more than twenty initial and advanced service schools where sailors were trained and prepared for the fleet. Some of these included the Machinists Mate school, Electronics school, Hospital Corpsman school, Gunners Mate school, Quartermaster school, and Divers school. The following day I checked in and immediately I received my orders. I was assigned as Personnelman in the U.S. Navy Seabee training school. This would be my home until discharge day.

Once again I was blessed. My new assignment was great, as I would not be living in the base barracks. At the school we had private rooms for instructors and staff who were not living off-base with their dependents. This was excellent! In my duties, I would handle the records and processing of the new students (both regular Navy and

Reservists) and prepare the curriculum from the lesson plans provided by the instructors. The Seabee school was located about ten miles from the Training Center. We had experienced Seabee instructors teaching the students in the field of heavy equipment, surveying, carpentry, and plumbing. By this time I already had the rank of Petty Officer 2nd class in Personnel. Not too bad a grade for less than five years service. I was given a jeep to travel to and from the base, to attend meetings, and of course the mess hall. I really enjoyed my work and the personnel I worked with. In my official duties I reported directly to Commander James Cross, in charge of the school, and a World War II veteran of the Seabees.

Commander Cross had connections with the big brass at the Schlitz Brewery in Milwaukee. About every six weeks the staff of the Seabee school and some guests had a big dinner party in the recreation hall of the brewery. The Irish might call it a soiree, to a sailor it was a blast. There was plenty of food, beer, and music, everything courtesy of Schlitz. This gathering was well liked by all the personnel of the Seabee School. From time to time, Commander Cross would talk to me about staying in the Navy. My pay grade was E-5 and a 2nd Class Petty Officer. He figured that I could attain E-7 or Chief Petty Officer in less than five years. This sounded very difficult to achieve, but Commander Cross was trying hard to re-enlist me. My plans however, were different.

In the meantime I had other things happening to me in Great Lakes. In a first for me, I received orders for weekend Shore Patrol duty in downtown Chicago. Being a 2nd Class Petty Officer I was now eligible for Shore Patrol. For the first time in my Navy career I carried a weapon, a billy club, and had a black and yellow band on my right arm with the letters SP. They teamed me up with a veteran Chief Petty Officer who was well versed in shore patrol duties. The weather in downtown Chicago was not too favorable – a cold 18 degrees. As we walked the streets of Chicago our duties were the protection and the well-being of all sailors on the streets. That night it was so cold that we went inside the Chicago arena to warm up a bit. The Blackhawks were playing and it was the first time I ever saw a hockey game. I only had Shore Patrol duty twice in Great Lakes, but I enjoyed it. I went to Chicago often with my friends from the Seabee School. Chicago is also known as the "Windy City." It is a place of cultural institutions, art galleries, and museums. A few times I went to see the two baseball teams in Chicago: the Cubs in Wrigley Field and the White Sox in Comiskey Park. In downtown Chicago on the avenue known as the "Loop" there was a huge dance place known as the Trianon Ball Room. It was free admission if you wore the Navy uniform. The big bands and orchestras of that era were there. As far as I'm concerned, there will never be better music than Glenn Miller, Tommy Dorsey, Harry James, and Les Brown.

It was at Great Lakes that I participated in sports – fast-pitch softball and baseball. More on that later. Golf was not on the agenda yet. I purchased my first car also. It was a gray 1951 Chevrolet. For more than eight months I had a part-time job as short-order cook – can you imagine? – at the Officers Club. I stayed busy. I recall Dad always telling me that work is honorable. Additionally, I bought a complete set of oil painting materials; brushes, paints, palette, canvas, sketchpad, charcoal, et cetera. Surely, these items kept me busy during the cold winter months that I spent at Great Lakes, which was right next to frigid Lake Michigan.

Finally, departure time! My Navy time was up. After some snacks in the school lounge, Commander Cross presented me with my Navy Honorable Discharge and a few gifts from the staff. Among one of the gifts I received was a replica of a huge sign we had at the entrance of the Seabee School. It read: "For when we reach the isle of Japan, with our hats at a jaunty tilt, we'll enter the city of Tokyo, on the roads the Seabees built." This is a proud proverb of the Navy Seabees. Being known for building and fighting, the Seabees would admit and boast that they were building the roads for the Japanese to retreat on.

The following day I left the Great Lakes Naval Base; my destination – Laredo, Texas. My Navy time was over, civilian life was beginning and my journey continued.

1955 – Seabee School, U.S. Naval Training Center, Great Lakes, Illinois.

Chapter 14 – Back in Laredo – Reminiscing

It was good to be back in Laredo and to see Mom, Dad, and my family. Most certainly I would indulge in Mom's home-cooked Mexican delicacies. It was nice to get up early in the morning, walk around the orange and peach trees, pray, meditate, and reminisce. What beautiful memories penetrated the mind as I walked the terrain of my bygone days! What plans I had for my future were still concealed, unknown. At the moment I just reminisced. Such recollections are well worth calling to my mind.

- At the far end of my dad's property was a pomegranate – a granada tree. Next to it were the orange and peach trees. One evening when I was still a kid, Dad and I saw a young boy with his pockets full of oranges. He was probably around nine years old. He was so surprised; as he looked at us, he was scared-stiffed, frightened, and wouldn't speak a word. Dad told him, "Don't you ever do that again. The next time you want oranges you come to the front door and see me and I'll give you all the oranges you want." The kid was smaller than me (get a rope!) and I was sure I could handle him. I told Dad, "I can take care of him!" Quickly Dad tells me: "I'll take care of you later – be quiet." The little boy left. Immediately I knew that this was another of my Dad's acts of forgiveness and generosity. *"A generous man will be blessed for he shares his food with the poor.* (Proverbs 22:9)

- Outside on the back of the store, under the shade of a chinaberry (*una lila*) tree, we had a small storage room where sacks of Purina, corn, and beans were stored. One early morning, Dad found the door and lock broken and two sacks of Purina missing. Hastily he called the sheriff's office. In no time at all, two deputies arrived and began their investigation. And Holy Moses, what an investigation! Now, please read this prudently. As I write this, I still can't believe it – but I am laughing. From the deputy who conducted the investigation, these were his words: "*Señor Díaz, despues del estudio y el analisis del robo, el resultado es que los rateros entraron por esta puerta.*" Translated, it means this: "Mr. Díaz, after our study and analysis of the theft, our conclusion is that the thieves came in through this door." If you had never seen Dad angry, let me say that he was boiling mad. He took a deep breath (or maybe two) then he said: "*Bola de brutos y pendejos, solo hay una puerta!*" "You bunch of stupid jerks, there's only one door." I venture to say that my dad never got back the two sacks of Purina.

- My son David was already five years old when he liked to run races with my dad. They would run around the orange trees, from one end of the property to the driveway. However, David could never win a race. On one occasion as we were coming back to San Antonio, he told me in a serious tone: "Dad, do you know why I can never beat Grandpa? It's because he wears those crazy tennis shoes!" The crazy tennis shoes he was referring to were the famous high tops. In my childhood days those were the only type you could buy and you could get a good pair for $2.39. Now, you see grossly overpriced tennis shoes at prices of up to $300.00.

- Have you ever heard about the treasure of Pancho Villa? Many legends or *leyendas* and stories have been told of Pancho Villa and his buried treasure. Throughout South Texas among Hispanic communities you hear of different sites or locations where this wealth may be buried. Hearsay and rumors had it that not too far from my parent's house there was a small abandoned shack in the brush where that gold could be hidden. So one day, three ten-year-old Sherlock Holmes boy detectives decided to conduct a full investigation and thorough search for that gold. It was said that once a month from a distance you could see flames inside that shack. Late one night the three detectives began the hunt. Two of my friends came to my house and quietly knocked outside the window of my bedroom. I unhooked the *aldaba* (window latch) from the screen door, got out, and we were on our way. We were of course very scared as we neared the shack; more so as I opened the squeaking door. We lit some matches. There was a dirt-floored kitchen and another small room. We found a large red book, nearly two feet in size, by the chimney. In the book were old photos from WWI. We searched and dug inside the shack but to our disgust we found nothing – no signs of the treasure of the famous bandit, Pancho Villa. Finally, we were assured and confident that there was none of his treasure in our neck of the woods. There were no further searches.

- You will find them in every city or town around the country. I am referring to the names, nicknames, or labels given to neighborhoods. In my travels around the country this is so prevalent. I don't know the source or the origin, or who on earth comes up with a name for their barrios or neighborhoods. In Laredo this has been the custom, and some of the neighborhood names are real humdingers – absurd and comical. Since my childhood days in Laredo, some of the barrio names have not changed. For example:

  El barrio del Azteca – (Aztec)
  El barrio del Cuatro – (Four)
  El barrio de Cantaranas (where the frogs sing or croak)
  El barrio de las Cruzes (the Crosses)

El barrio de la Ladrillera (the Brickyard)
El barrio de Guadalupe
 (where Our Lady of Guadalupe church is located)
El barrio de Sal si Puedes (Come out if you can)
El barrio de Los Amores (Lovers)
El barrio de Santo Niño (the Holy Child)
El barrio del Puente Blanco (the White Bridge)

What an array of barrio assignments! Another thing, I don't even know the boundary for each barrio. Some years ago I was talking to my brother-in-law, Pete Tovar, who worked for the Central Power & Light Company of Laredo. Being that he was familiar with the geography of Laredo, I asked him just what barrio I belonged to. I've always thought that I resided in *El barrio de Guadalupe*. Pete told me, "You live in *El barrio de los Amores*." I don't know if that's good or bad, but my brother-in-law switched me from a Holy barrio to a Loving barrio. Meditate on that?

There is no holiday like Christmas. As far back as I remember, Christmas in Laredo was a time for families to reunite and be grateful for all that they had. The world has changed tremendously since my childhood days. Perhaps as I have grown older I have become fatigued or wearied with so much materialism, shopping, and hurriedness that accompanies Christmas. But the real meaning of the spirit of Christmas remains. No one has said it better than the angel's magnificent proclamation to the shepherds. Saint Luke, the third gospel author of the New Testament was inspired to write: *"You have nothing to fear! I come to proclaim good news to you."* (Luke 2: 10) In these thirteen words, Saint Luke summarizes the beginning of the greatest event that has occurred in the history of humanity. And what are the great news Luke is calling attention to? It is that a Savior has been born. It is the Messiah in the form of a baby which has come into the world. I love history. But I'll guarantee you that in all the history books of the world we will never find an event as great, important, and beautiful as the one in the gospel of Luke. *"You have nothing to fear! I come to proclaim good news to you."* When is the last time you heard something like that? When is the last time you heard something good and refreshing? At the moment there is not much good news on television, and the newspapers seldom give you anything pleasant or godly to read. Practically everything that you see on TV and read in the newspapers is about crime, violence, drugs, wars, disease, families breaking apart, divorces, delinquency, and gangs. Society and our families are surrounded with disappointments, anxieties, and failures. That good news that the angel proclaimed then still applies to us now. A savior is born and He is our hope. He is the answer, because man alone can do nothing by himself. We are useless without that infant child in the manger. That child has been the hope of my life and you know what? Nothing is impossible for Him.

In Laredo and the Hispanic culture there are a number of religious festivities associated with Christmas and the child Jesus. The Spanish missionaries introduced *Las Posadas*. This is the Christmas drama that represents Joseph and Mary seeking lodging to prepare for the birth of Jesus. (Luke 2: 1-14) There is another play or drama called *La Pastorela*. This is a traditional Spanish pageant that describes the shepherd's journey to Bethlehem. A *pastorela* can last from two to three hours. The play itself is a struggle with evil, and an invitation to do good. Out of the many Christmas plays and festivities, I suppose my favorite is *La Acostada del Niño Dios*. It means the "Laying Down of the Child Jesus in the Cradle." Even though I say that this play is my favorite, I didn't care much to be a participant. Maybe it was always my favorite because there were so many goodies and sweets after the ceremony. This play takes place on Christmas Eve and is done in Spanish-speaking homes. After the play we would go immediately to *la misa de gallo* or midnight Mass. I'll describe part of this beautiful Christmas religious play since it is still so vividly stamped in my memory.

My grandmother Gabriela and a lady by the name of Micaéla were the organizers of *La Acostada del Niño Dios*. It began with Christmas songs, followed by prayers. Sometimes the recitation of the Rosary was said along with the litany of the Virgin Mary and the singing of some hymns. The liturgy was well-composed, the emphasis being the laying of the baby Jesus in the cradle. One more thing, the Three Kings came into the picture also. (No buts about it; I never liked this part of the play.) The Three Kings, boys about six or seven years old, were neatly and skillfully dressed. One of the Kings supposedly was black, and the child portraying him had his face and hands daubed with charcoal. As kids no one liked this. Some even pretended to be sick so as not to participate in the play. Nonetheless, the show must go on. The Three Kings approached the elegant and sacred nativity scene and presented the gifts of frankincense, gold, and myrrh to the baby Jesus. May I say here that *La Acostada del Niño Dios* and the *Pastorela* are not Biblical, according to the account of the Gospel of Matthew 2: 1. The Bible account of Matthew does not specify the number of Kings, nor the names of Melchior, Gaspar, and Balthazar. This is only tradition or a legend handed down by Spanish missionaries.

How well I remember the nativity scene and the altar – the design and the creative work of art was magnificent. All of it was handmade, beginning with the rolling countryside, the trees, birds, rocks, and the distant small houses on the hills. It was a sight to behold. Immediately after the play and before departing for midnight mass came what I believed to be the most important function of the whole evening. It was hot chocolate, homemade cookies, tamales, *buñuelos,* and other goodies. After this, we all walked to Our Lady of Guadalupe church for midnight mass.

Outside the house, just before leaving for church, there was a short prayer of thanksgiving. Even as a child, on our way to the church I felt so much peace and joy. I could sense that there was an abundance of happiness and harmony present. Every Christmas Eve this joyful event is present in my mind. Remember that this was shortly after the Depression years, and there was still poverty and need. However, the Spirit of God was there. The child Jesus was present and the star was leading us to the bliss and the gratification that comes to those who love and serve our Creator God.

Chapter 15 – The Two-Dollar Bet –
My First Civil Service Job

I am sure that most of you, particularly veterans of the Armed Forces, have heard of Master Sgt. Roy P. Benavidez from Cuero, Texas. After the Vietnam War he was awarded the nations' highest military decoration; the Congressional Medal of Honor. Benavidez is one of the 44 Hispanics nationwide who has earned this high honor. In his book *Medal of Honor: One Man's Journey from Poverty and Prejudice,* he writes the following: "I believe that there is no greater calling for a man or woman to serve in the military of a free nation. I believe that it is a calling that transcends all others because embedded deep within the soul of every free man or woman is the knowledge that every freedom we have was earned for us by our ancestors, who paid some price for that freedom."

I was glad to be in Laredo once again and proud that I had honorably served my country. Other Laredoans were also returning home from Korea, but some of my friends did not make it back. There are times when I go to Laredo that I visit the markers or monuments in Jarvis Plaza where veterans who gave their lives in all the wars are remembered. As I stand in front of the Korean monument I read with teary eyes the names of my school friends who gave their lives defending our country. Among them are Amado Leal, Paz Frausto, and Luis Ibarra. Luis was active in Boy's Club sports. Luis and I played basketball and our team won the Teenage Basketball League championship for two years. Also, Luis and I were the Laredo teenage doubles champions in table tennis. Our Boys Club coach, Joe Prieto, wrote a remarkable article in the *Laredo Times* after Luis was killed in action in Korea. In this article that I still have, Coach wrote: "He was the one I could really count on when the chips were down in all kinds of sports and the first one to show leadership characteristics. He was the first one to learn how to swim in the Boy's Club pool, and the first one to make the All Star Basketball team in the Teen-age league and the first one to be voted the most improved player in the League. He was the first Boys Club member to join the 1st Marine Division and the first Boys Club member to die for his country." I really admired Luis. He never gave up. In San Diego, California, I saw Luis a few days before we set sail on the same convoy for Korea.

It was decision-making time for me. What's next? Should I look for a job, or go to college? At this time, Korean veterans had a few benefits, like the Veterans Land Program for buying a home and the G. I. Bill for education. Another benefit was one called the 26/26. This meant that for 26 weeks you would receive $26 each week. Sometimes you heard some of the veterans say: "Well, so what are you doing now?" The reply was: *"Le estoy pegando al los 26,"* or I'm hitting or using the $26. These benefits were given to compensate Korean veterans for their wartime service. My decision finally, was to go to college under the G. I. Bill and so I enrolled in Laredo Junior College.

As was the case for WWII veterans, tuition was no longer paid directly to the chosen college or university. Instead, the Korean veterans received a monthly fixed amount to use for their tuition fees and books. As a Navy veteran I used the G. I. Bill to the fullest extent of my education. Contrary to the opinion of many people, the G. I. Bill usually would not pay for all college expenses. I only remained in Laredo Junior College for half a year. Why? It was because of a $2.00 bet. Let me explain. After my discharge, I was living in my childhood home with Mom and Dad. Some of my friends came to see me once in while. Among them was Ernesto Peña, who served in the Air Force and lived just a few houses away.

One evening we were discussing what we were going to do after serving in the military. He mentioned that Lackland and Kelly AFB in San Antonio were hiring veterans. I thought about it for a while. Why on earth shouldn't I go to San Antonio? I was not married and just out of the Navy . . . no problems. Later Ernesto suggested, "Let's go to San Antonio and take an entrance exam for a job." It sounded good to me. With a little more than five years of naval service, I could apply this Navy time to a Federal retirement. In any case, there was a challenge in the form of a bet. Ernesto came out and said to me: "I bet you two dollars that I pass the entrance exam in San Antonio and you don't."

Easy money, I thought. The bet was on.

In a few weeks we were on the way to the Alamo city. We took the entrance exam at the Federal Building on Houston Street, which was at the time, the main Post Office in San Antonio. In about three weeks I received a letter from Kelly AFB saying that I had passed the exam and I had a job waiting . . . report in ten days! Just like that! As my friend Ernesto handed me the two-dollar wager money, I could see he wasn't too cheerful, since he had flunked the test. But he still wanted to work in San Antonio. About six months later I saw Ernesto there; he was driving an ambulance. So now, of all things, I had a job in what was to be my future home, San Antonio. The Lord sure works in mysterious ways.

My position – my first job in Civil Service was in the Personnel section of the Directorate of Supply. The work was easy for me. I handled more than fifty personnel records for a packing section. Every two weeks I would pass out their paychecks. I also kept track of the section productivity charts. But my new job would only last one year. I was moving. My journey continued.

Just before leaving the *USS Antietam*, the chaplain had talked to me about applying for entrance to the Maryknoll College in

Brookline, Massachusetts. This was a novitiate for the Brothers of Maryknoll and I would be in their one-year-long program. After my resignation from Civil Service, I departed for Maryknoll College where I studied for one year. Again, I was using my G. I. Bill. The campus of Maryknoll was so beautiful and secluded. I could tell that it benefited my spiritual life immensely. I loved all the subjects that were being taught in Maryknoll. Also, there was manual labor we had to perform, as well as daily mass, prayers, and spiritual exercises that we had to accomplish. I thought it was a strict schedule that we followed. For most of the day, in our classes, in our manual labor, and especially during our religious devotions, there was silence. I loved the silence.

Soon, my one year of studies came to an end at Maryknoll. I came back to San Antonio where I returned to work in Civil Service. I was so pleased with my education at Maryknoll and in addition, my semester hours were accumulating. The Base Housing office was my next place of employment at Kelly AFB. It was a job with a bit of pressure and stress. I collected and kept track of the rental fees for all the Air Force personnel living in base housing at Kelly AFB. Among other things, two or three days a week I was attending night classes at Saint Mary's University and San Antonio College. Also I had joined the U.S. Naval Reserve, which required me to attend training one night a week. Let me say here, I did not have to perform any more duties for the Navy, as I had served more than five years already. But as a 2nd Class Petty Officer there was a quarterly salary, and two weeks of training duty pay every year.

Here's a point of interest for you veterans of the Army and Air Force who are reservists and perform your two-weeks-a-year training duty. For your annual two-week duty you most likely traveled together as a unit, or regiment, or squadron on a specified date given to you by your superiors. I know some of the Army reservists here in

San Antonio still travel by truck to Fort Hood or Camp Bullis for their training. Here is how the Navy did it; I could go on my annual training duty whatever time of the year I wanted to go, I could select whatever ship or station I wanted, be it East coast or West coast, and I could travel whatever method I wanted – by plane, my own car, train, or bus. How do you like those apples?

Between my job at Kelly AFB, my night college classes, and my Navy Reserve duties, somehow I still found the time to frequently travel to Laredo to see my girlfriend. I was now dating my 1st grade friend and later my bride and wife . . . Yolanda.

1956 – Maryknoll College, Brookline, Massachusetts.

Chapter 16 – Marriage and My Children

It is important that I mention the first dates with my future wife. Men, read this very carefully; I don't know if this is still practiced or not, but for some men, this custom might seem antiquated or archaic. The ground rules for dating my future wife were clear and to the point. Yes, I could date her, but she had to be home by 10:00 p.m. Yes, I said that right! I had to bring her home by 10:00 p.m. That was the law. No ifs or buts! Did I complain or gripe? What do you think? Let me put it this way; I followed the law.

Here's another of those so-called antiquated customs and traditions that a man ready for marriage went through. I sincerely believe that most men do not accept this now, but it was a must, back then. You had to face the music and ask the parents of the bride for her hand in marriage. The parents could refuse or tell you to come back later. Anyway, after all the pre-marital customs were completed, I married María Yolanda Lozano at Holy Redeemer Catholic Church in Laredo, Texas. It was a simple marriage, not much fanfare, and not much of the glamour, glitter, and noise that you usually have to endure in Hispanic weddings. That is precisely the way we wanted it. After the wedding there was a breakfast – and that was it. Can you believe this? There was no dance, no cantina music, no alcohol, or the rest of the shenanigans that you see in most weddings in South Texas. For our honeymoon, we traveled first to the San Juan Shrine in the Río Grande Valley and then to New Orleans, Louisiana. After that we settled in San Antonio.

Two years after we were married, Patricia, our first daughter was born. Then two years later our second daughter, Shirley, and three years later it was David, our son. How blessed and fortunate l am for my wonderful family. Undeniably, this was truly a gift from God. In my early morning devotions of the *Liturgy of the Hours* I have never forgotten to thank my Creator for this divine family blessing he bestowed on me. There was in me a sense of joy and admiration as I saw my wife teaching and training our children during their infancy and in the early stages of their lives. Her patience and devotion to the children was quite impressive. As the Latin saying goes: *"Tempus fugit"* or "time flies." All three of the kids finished their high school studies. Patty graduated from Saint Francis Catholic High School; Shirley and David graduated from Luther Burbank High School.

As stated before, Holy Redeemer Catholic Church, where we were married, was my wife's parish, while I belonged to Our Lady of Guadalupe. As I go back to 1957, the year of my marriage, I can bring to mind many recollections of the events and incidents of that wonderful day. First of all, the day of our marriage was the 20th of October. Why that date? Because my wife's mother and grandmother were married on that day. The marriage date was fine with me.

Here's a question for you ladies: are all brides late for their wedding? By late, I mean five, fifteen, or twenty minutes late. Statistics tell us that over 20 per cent of the brides are late arrivals for their nuptials. Well, my wife was late for her wedding – maybe fifteen minutes late. For two or three days before the wedding she was suffering from her teenage nemesis . . . gall-bladder problems. Consequently, because the bride was late for the wedding, the congregation had to wait, the priest had to wait, and last but not least the eager and anxious groom had to wait. As the waiting went on, I was in the sacristy of the church with the priest and my younger brother Beto, who was the best man. The priest, a grumpy Spanish Oblate, was already fuming. Finally he got after my brother for the bride's delay and he was really chewing him out. You see, he thought my brother was the groom. Meanwhile I went to the corner of the sacristy, giggling and laughing up a storm. Poor Manito. (Little brother) But now, listen to this! Who would ever imagine that thirty-one years later in this same church of Holy Redeemer in Laredo, Texas, and in the same sacristy, as an ordained Deacon of the Catholic Church, I would be dressing in my alb, stole, and dalmatic, to assist the Agustinian priests at the altar and to preach English and Spanish homilies. For sure, I never imagined this! Who knows the ways and the plans of God? *"Can you penetrate the designs of God? Dare you view the perfection of the Almighty?"* (Job 11: 7)

My wife's family was an added blessing for me. My in-laws were a devout and unselfish couple whom I respected so much. They also were very considerate and amiable to me. The young lady that I was marrying was a devout Roman Catholic and a faithful Christian. On one occasion, my sister Carmen labeled her as "the woman from the book of Proverbs." So we entered gladly and in a Christ-like manner into the holy sacrament of marriage. My spouse would be always, next to God, my number one love in my life. In our 43 years of marriage we have treated each other with respect, dignity, and equality. My wife and I cherished life as we believed in the sacredness of life. And as we grew in our marriage vows we taught our children the values of life and the love for God. Thank you again, Lord, for the woman of my life.

In my Bible classes that I taught, and the homilies that I preached on the sacredness of the marriage sacrament, I often cited a special wedding that I performed in my parish in San Antonio. During the sermon I told the couple to be married that they would give their word and promise to each other, and to God. This promise was to be true and faithful to each other in good times and in bad times, and in sickness and in health. They were to love and honor each other for the rest of their lives. This is a sacred promise: a vow before almighty God. *"Con Dios no se juega."* *"You don't play with God."* This vow, this promise is also a covenant between husband and wife and God.

By the way, the groom was an algebra teacher at nearby John F. Kennedy High School.

In the wedding homily, I also mentioned that we would put aside the rules of algebra. Instead, I said that one major rule in marriage would be $1 + 1 = 1$; not what algebra tells us, $1 + 1 = 2$. After today, the man and woman in marriage would be one. Everything would be one and belong to both of you. Everything would be one . . . your home, car, checking account, your dreams, your plans, and your goals. Everything would belong to both of you, except one thing: the toothbrush. You will still use your own toothbrush! The two of you are now one. Twice in scripture, our Lord warns us and tells us very clear: *"For this reason a man shall leave his father and mother, and shall cling to his wife, and the two shall be one."* (Genesis 2: 24) (Ephesians 5: 31)

This then is how my wife and I, with the help of God, lived our married life, and that is that the two of us are one. Please understand that in this world there are no perfect marriages. Nothing is perfect in this world. Marriages are not perfect, society is not perfect, the schools are not perfect, the church is not perfect, and for sure the government is not perfect. During your marriage covenant you will have moments in your life when everything will not be a bed of roses, when things will not be so lovey-dovey. Be assured that there will be problems, sufferings, tears, sorrows, and many afflictions. But I have some good news for you.

Whenever these problems come, when you are going through despair and grief in you married life, I'm going to refer you to a counselor. I would urge you to seek the advice of the greatest counselor the world has ever known. As a matter of fact, the prophet Isaiah called Him *"Wonder Counselor."* (Isaiah 9: 5) He can solve any marriage problem, and He can cure any suffering and wipe away all tears. He knows how to do it because He is the inventor of marriage. He created the groom and the bride; He knows all their thoughts and understands all of their problems. His name is Jesus Christ of Nazareth, and He is the King of Kings, and Lord of Lords, and He is the Wonder Counselor.

Let me persuade you that when you are loaded with stress and overburdened with the pressures of life, call on Him and he will comfort you. He will give you the guidance and he will enlighten you. Call on him – talk to him, share with him your joys and your disappointments. Share with the Wonder Counselor your failures and your victories and your blessings. He is always available. He does not keep regular office hours. He is available twenty-four hours a day, seven days a week. He is always ready to listen to your marriage problems, and best of all his services are free, because you are his children. He loves you and he cares for you. Your Wonder Counselor will always be generous and forgiving; he loves you and me so much, regardless of what we have done. For the many times that we have offended him, He loves us; for the many times we have failed him, He loves us; for the many times we have been unfaithful to him, He loves us. He loves you and me so much that He stretched out his arms on the cross and he died for us. That is real love. Has anyone ever done that for you or for me? No – nobody! During my married life I have been blessed with so many gifts and graces from the Wonder Counselor. My marriage continued to grow in the love and service for God. My wish is that these same blessings will come to you in your married life. Remember, we are useless without Him, but with God, all things are possible. Love Him and trust in Him.

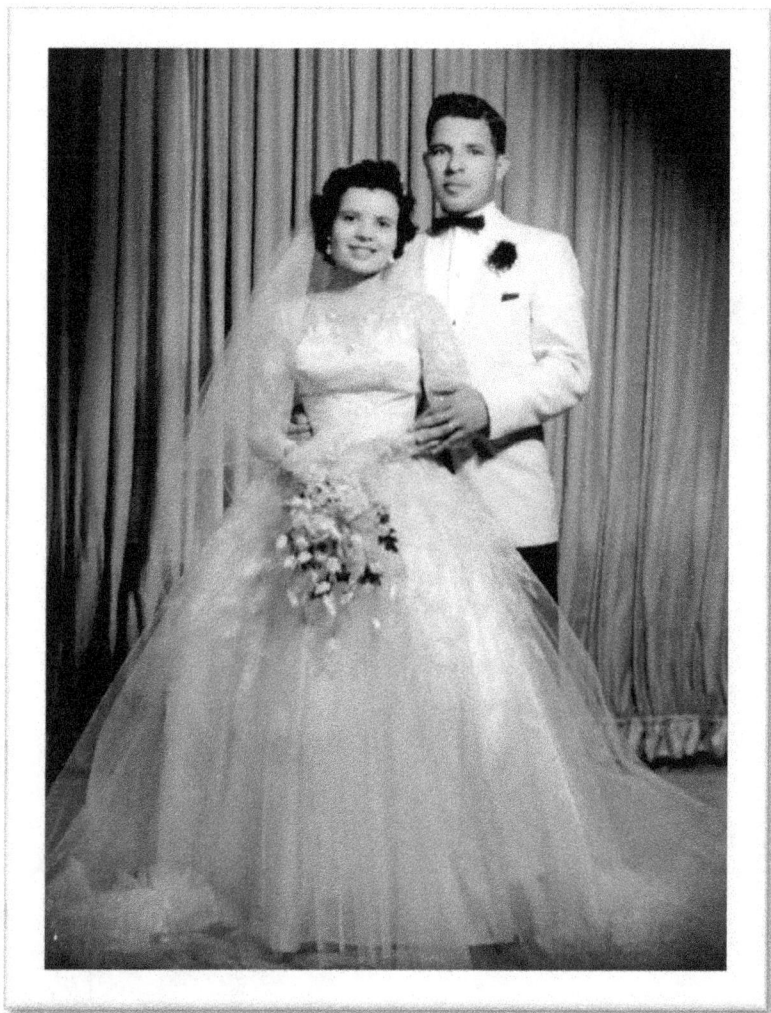

Our wedding, October 20, 1957.

My daughter Patricia.

*My daughter
Shirley.*

My son David.

Chapter 17 – My Golf Tour of the 50 States – *Ripley's Believe It Or Not*

"Golf is a temporary insanity practiced on a pasture."
– Dave Kindred

In 1966, I started playing the absurd and ridiculous game of golf. (I love it!) I was a member of the Metropolitan Golf Association, where I first played competitive golf in San Antonio. In my first four years with this club, my handicap dropped from a 14 to a 3. We played golf courses in and around the city. Additionally, I was playing different courses in my travels around the country – be it my vacations, my work travels, or when I went to my Navy reunions. I started listing all the different golf courses and also keeping a scorecard for each course that I played. Presently I have played 323 different golf courses in the United States, Canada, and Mexico, and have played golf in each of the 50 states.

For this accomplishment, I appeared in *Ripley's Believe it or Not* on June 8, 2001. I wrote a book and titled it *My Golf Tour of the 50 States*. All the golf courses that I have played are listed alphabetically by state in my booklet, and I included incidents that I observed in and around golf links. There is a page in this book where I have recorded my five prettiest golf courses, my five ugliest, my five easiest, and my five toughest golf courses. Some ladies in the rectory of my parish, Saint John Berchmans, admonished me for printing in my book that Texas has the five ugliest golf courses, but in my defense I say also that Texas has some of the most beautiful courses in the country.

Some years back I was riding in a hearse to do a graveside service in San Fernando Cemetery Number 2, just north of my parish. Driving the hearse was Monty, the funeral director and a good friend of mine for many years, whom I had met through my church ministry. Monty came up with an interesting observation. He told me: "You know Deacon, you would be a rich man if you had five dollars for every mile you have traveled around the country and around the world. And don't forget to add the miles you have traveled in a hearse to the cemeteries in San Antonio and surrounding areas!" Later I gave this careful consideration.

Let's see, twice across the Pacific Ocean, the many sea exercises and maneuvers we had out of San Diego and Pearl, plus the many miles in a hearse. (As an ordained Deacon I have done over two hundred graveside services.) Add to that my travels around the United States, Canada, and Mexico. Yes, the mileage is immense and at five dollars a mile – Wow! Monty has already retired but if space permits and if my 39-year-old mind (?) doesn't forget, I'll include an original and humorous incident about him in a later chapter.

As written in my golf book, I found traveling inspiring and unforgettable. Traveling is an adventure and a distinctive type of an education. To travel is to be free, to seek special places that refresh us and revive us. Our great country, the United States, offers so many of these places to visit. The Lone Star State of Texas alone has so many beautiful sites to visit; from its cosmopolitan cities to the lakes country, mountains, seashores, rolling woodlands, and the rugged brush country of South Texas that I deeply love. Many people still prefer to travel abroad. I do not understand the logic of this, because America has it all. And as I have traveled intensively, there is so much to view in the picturesque beauty and vastness of our country. Among some of the beautiful areas that I have seen and visited in the United States are these:

They call the Blue Ridge Parkway one of America's most scenic drives. It is a spectacular view as you follow the mountain crests of the Shenandoah National Park in Virginia, to the Great Smoky

Mountains in North Carolina and Tennessee. What beauty there is in the colorful wilderness and mountain forests!

To me, the Rocky Mountain region offers the most panoramic landscapes in the United States. While crossing the majestic Beartooth Pass from northern Wyoming into Montana, I saw and I named it God's creation, at its best. The Sioux Indians called this scenic pass "The Highway to Heaven." It is 60 miles of breathtaking highway at 11,000 feet above sea level. The speed limit sometimes is five to ten miles per hour. As you look down there are smaller mountains below, broad valleys, and amazing peaks. Its alpine meadows and glass-clear lakes are part of the 800,000 acres of wilderness just north of the Yellowstone National Park. What a sight . . . enough to take your breath away!

I marveled at the bold land of the Apaches and the enduring desert sun in the great states of Arizona and New Mexico. These two states have so many cultural, historical, and recreational attractions. Of course, Arizona is one of the country's top golf vacation destinations.

In western Maryland, near the town of Sharpsburg, there is a stream called Antietam Creek. The area is so peaceful and serene. But it wasn't peaceful on that bloody day of September 17, 1862, when two great armies collided there. They were General Robert E. Lee's Army of Northern Virginia against General George McClellan's Army of the Potomac. When the September sun finally set upon that devastated battlefield, more than 22,000 Americans had fallen in a single day. Antietam was the single bloodiest day of the Civil War. During my Navy tour of duty I served on two aircraft carriers . . . the *USS Badoeng Strait* and the *USS Antietam*. I will always be proud of the shared legacy – a remarkable fighting warship named after a famous Civil War battle – Antietam. In the more than 30 annual Antietam Association Ship's reunions that I have attended, we have met three times in Sharpsburg, Maryland. As chaplain of the Association, one year I was doing a memorial service in the Antietam battlefield itself! This happens to me very seldom but as I was speaking from the podium, facing my shipmates and the battlefield, I suddenly became sorrow-stricken and almost broke down. The quiet Maryland countryside in Antietam Creek remains in my mind as the most solemn and venerable site in the United States. One important historical point to remember here is that soon after the famous battle of Antietam, President Abraham Lincoln issued the historic Emancipation Proclamation.

In my beloved brush country of South Texas, it is not uncommon to see cattle crossing and deer crossing signs. You will notice these signs in state and county roads all over Texas. Once I saw an elk crossing sign, just east of Port Angeles, Washington. This city, located in north Washington State is near the famous Strait of Juan de Fuca, which separates the United States and Victoria, British Columbia, Canada. Then in the early 70's I attended a Budget/Auditing seminar at the Rock Island Army Arsenal in the Quad Cities in Iowa. Just north of Davenport, I saw a duck crossing. This was a shocker for me. However, the crossing that took the cake was the turtle crossing I saw on the island of Maui, Hawaii. I could not believe it! As you travel the spectacular south road from Lahaina to Wailea then on to Highway 310 you will witness the amazing "turtle crossing." I just had to take some photos. Left of the highway is the Kealia fish pond. From this pond a multitude of turtles, big and small, cross the highway on their way to the Pacific Ocean. It is just unbelievable and incredible. So much for the crossings.

The Arkansas National "7 Byway" is one of America's ten most scenic roads. Most likely you have read about this route in travel guides and magazines. As you travel this road, it climbs, plunges, and twists through two national forests. You will also see lakes, winding rivers, and pretty scenery. From IH 30 East, I cut north in Arkadelphia, Arkansas, and stayed on Highway 7. My destination was Branson, Missouri. My favorite spots on this highway were the Arkansas Grand Canyon and the Dardenelle, an area know for its beautiful trees. I will never forget the tranquil communities with such names as Coon Skin Springs, Booger Hollow, Moccasin Gap, and Dog Patch . . . here I am sure lives the peaceful spirit of the Ozarks.

After traveling and visiting the 50 states in America and six countries, where then is my prettiest place? What place, what site is the most enchanted and charming that I have seen? It was certainly a difficult choice to make . . . but here it is:

Number 3 – Antietam National Battlefield, Sharpsburg, Maryland
Number 2 – Zion National Park, Southwestern Utah
Number 1 – Grand Teton National Park, Jackson Hole, Wyoming

Not only is my prettiest place the Teton National Park in Wyoming but my prettiest golf course is also there. I had a hard time concentrating on my golf game as I played the Teton Pines Country Club. This attractive golf course overlooks the picturesque Grand Teton mountain range. Those mountain peaks were always staring at me. You cannot keep your eyes away from them – just try. You just can't – those mountains are magnetically beautiful. On a clear morning you will see their real beauty. A mighty river flows through the valley below – the Snake River. How glorious is the scenery around this river; an abundance of beautiful flowers, trees, birds, and wild animals. This then is the view of the Grand Teton National Park. Come and see it and you will like it. I did! In the quiet evenings at home in my back patio, on the golf courses and while traveling the roads in South Texas, I still see them . . . and they are looking at me. They are clearly visible, even now – the peaks of the Grand Tetons. I know they will remain close to me – of this I am certain.

It is so breathtaking and inspiring, each time I look at a map of the United States. The map looks so huge. The United States of America has an area of four million square miles. Only Russia, Canada, and China are larger in area. With this in mind, my golf tour of America looks majestic and impressive. I am fortunate and grateful for the accomplishment of playing golf in all the 50 States. My thanks and appreciation go first to the good Lord for giving me the time, my health, and the resources to realize this golf tour.

My sincere thanks and a tip of the golf cap and two mulligans also go to the following golfers. They took me to play so many golf courses in their neck of the woods. I am much obliged to my son-in-law Rick García for guiding me around the Dallas area, and my other son-in-law Sammy Monge for doing the same in Fort Worth; my brother Chalo for showing me the golf courses around Houston, brother-in-law Stan Myslinski in Las Vegas, and finally my old shipmate and friend Tony Marasco, who showed me around the courses around Pittsburgh, Pennsylvania, and in Ohio.

On October of 2012, Laredo's Max Mandel Municipal Golf Course opened for play. Designed by Robert Trent Jones, one of the great golf architects in the country, this elegant course was very much needed in Laredo and South Texas. This gem of a course is where friendly service makes golfers feel at home. Four or five holes play alongside the historic Río Grande River. I believe that there is nothing a golfer wants more than a fun and challenging course, and you will find this at the "Max." The golf course is located northwest of Laredo on the Mines Road. (Highway 1472) Come and play – you will enjoy it.

Great! Keep your head down and follow through!

1969 – Member and Treasurer,
Metropolitan Golf Association,
San Antonio, Texas.

1972 – "A" Flight 2nd
place, Metropolitan
Association, San
Antonio, Texas.

Chapter 18 – The Meaning of Work

There's an old Spanish proverb that reads: *"El cementerio esta lleno de flojos y de tragónes."* "The cemetery is full of lazy ones and gluttons."

If I would ask five persons for the definition of work, most likely I would receive five different answers. Nevertheless, I think most of the answers would be correct. Work is an exertion or an effort directed to produce or accomplish something. You can also say that work is to be employed so as to earn a living. Work is a task, a job, or a position. As far back as I remember, I have worked. I have been employed in many different jobs. It is good to say that all eight of us in the family, four boys and four girls, were also employed as youngsters. This is great, but nowadays you don't see this in many families. I remember so well that Dad used to tell me that work is honorable and that work is necessary.

The great apostle Saint Paul was inspired to write: "If a man won't work, neither let him eat." (2nd Thessalonians 3:10) My younger sister, Irma, who resides in Las Vegas has her own rendition of this Bible passage. She says, *"El que no jale que no trage."* Now, some of you might not agree with me, but a man who doesn't work is a poor excuse for being a man. Yet, you still see so many people being provided with food, shelter, clothing, et cetera. Maybe I am getting into the political arena now, but being lazy is uncalled for.

Some of my jobs and tasks since my childhood days are listed in this chapter:

Shoeshine boy: it was the beginning of WWII and Laredo had two military bases, Fort McIntosh Army Base and the Laredo Army Air Corps Gunnery School. Many soldiers spent time around Jarvis Plaza and some needed shoeshines.

I sold lemons just outside of Kress Five and Ten Cent Store at the corner of Hidalgo and Convent Streets in the heart of downtown Laredo. Five of us kids would buy crates of lemons and sell them for about five or ten cents a dozen.

I delivered the *San Antonio Light* in the Heights area of Laredo.

I washed the huge front windows and swept the sidewalk of the fancy Bon Ton ladies store in Laredo, which catered to the affluent, and ran errands.

I worked as dishwasher at the elegant La Paloma restaurant, where I worked with two of the Luna brothers who were outstanding baseball players. After dishwashing, I was promoted to waiter. This is the first time that I wore a white shirt and black tie – and the tips were excellent.

I worked as membership clerk at the newly-opened Boys Club of Laredo. This was in a building which formerly housed the USO, so Laredo had the honor of having the biggest Boys Club in the country. My job here was after school and Saturdays. Additionally, I got to participate in sports events like basketball, swimming, and table tennis.

During the summers of the mid-1940's I delivered ice. Ice was a booming business in Laredo as many homes still did not have refrigerators. Mr. Mata, the owner of the ice house and restaurant, drove the ice truck, with me and another guy doing the deliveries. How well I remember! Pete would carry the 50-pound blocks of ice and I would carry the 25-pound blocks. For that time I can really say that the salary was exceptional; $19.50 a week. I would hand my mother the weekly salary. From this I would get about a dollar and fifty cents, with which I went to see the powerful Nuevo Laredo La Junta AAA baseball team, with enough money left for raspas and hamburgers. The dollar could buy plenty; let me repeat, this was a generous salary then.   Many years later in one of my Economics classes at San Antonio College, I prepared a monetary and financial study on the buying power of the dollar for the mid-1940's. Just imagine how much you could buy with four dollars at Dad's store in the years 1930 to 1940. Just imagine how much you can buy now, with twenty or thirty dollars at a supermarket.

While stationed at the U.S. Naval Training Center in Great Lakes, Illinois, I had a part-time job from 7:00 to 10:00 p.m., two days a week. I was a short-order cook at the base officer's club. My duties were cooking and serving hamburgers, fries, and sandwiches. Salary and tips were good. At times I would ask myself why I should work extra. I was already a 2nd Class Petty Officer and the salary wasn't that bad. Time permitting, I worked for about seven months. My boss, the club chef, once told me to consider a career in cooking or culinary art. No thank you! Can you just imagine me as a chef? For crying out loud, I don't know the difference between roasted, simmered, or broiled.

I have already made reference to my positions in federal service. I was assigned to the Directorate of Distribution. I worked as a production counter, then promoted to a position as workload control specialist, and finally ended my federal service career as a budget analyst in the War Plans and Programs office. During this time at Kelly AFB there were two jobs offered to me that I refused. First, I was accepted for a position with the Immigration and Naturalization Service, as it was known then. After I had passed the examination, Mr. Allan Skinner, the chief of the Laredo sector for the Immigration Service, wrote me and set up an interview. He was such a gracious man, and even gave me two extra weeks to think it over. It was a difficult decision to make, but eventually I decided to stay in my present job. It turned out for the best. Then another opportunity came up, when I was offered a job with promotion at our headquarters in

Wright Patterson Air Force Base in Dayton, Ohio. Again, I decided to remain in my present job.

And Dad, you were so right . . . "Work is honorable and necessary."

1972 – Just finishing my "Bluebonnets" oil painting.

Chapter 19 – Politics

"The reason they bury politicians 28 feet under is because deep down they're nice guys." – Anonymous

The definition of politics is still not very clear to me. Political experts tell us that politics is a method of decision-making for human beings and that politics is generally applied to government. Some people say that politicians are elected to serve the people and that there are two types of politicians – bad and crooked. I will not endanger myself in telling you what percent of politicians are crooked. You will find politics in social life, in the schools, in the church, in business, and of course the government. But politics is a way of life in America. Believe me, since its early founding, politics has been active in Laredo.

It may be that no one describes the early politics in Laredo quite as well as the great historian and teacher Kathleen DaCamara does in her book *Laredo on the Río Grande*. In this wonderful book she writes: "During the city election of 1886, the citizen's party was known as the 'Guaraches' and the other was the Democratic Party known as the 'Botas.' The Guaraches appealed mainly to the plebeian class, while the Botas appealed mainly to the aristocratic element. After a successful election the Botas planned a parade representing a mock funeral of the Guaraches. The Guaraches threatened violence if such a demonstration was undertaken. The Commanding Officer at Fort McIntosh had to send a body of U.S. soldiers to restore peace. By the following election all bitter feeling was healed, and the two parties joined to form the present Independent Party of Laredo which has been in power since that time." (*Laredo on the Río Grande*, pages 27-28)

Webb County, Duval County, and other counties in South Texas have been known historically for election irregularities and voter fraud. In Laredo you can still hear some rumbles of the *"partido viejo"* or the "old party." Stories are told of how dead people resurrected to vote in Laredo. As a youngster in Dad's store, I heard some stories about crooked elections. For example, it was said that during elections Laredo had more votes counted than Cleveland, Ohio. Why? Because they would say: "We have it made here; we have a cemetery in Laredo and one in Nuevo Laredo, Mexico." Election Day was when the dead people resurrected to go to the polls and vote – with a poll tax, of course. During an election day it was common to hear: *"Cuantas veces votaste?"* "How many times did you vote?" Well, just twice, that's enough. Or, how about the yarn that in Laredo, orphan children go to the polls during election days to wait for their dead parents to show up and vote. In the 1940's there was a young man in the neighborhood that used to brag about his policeman's pay. "I earn $24 a week," he would boast, "but on election days I have to bring five people to vote." Finally, the electronic age arrived in Laredo and voting machines were replacing the paper ballots. The story goes that for a few years the county kept rejecting the voting machines. But why? Unfortunately, they would say, the voting machines know how to count right.

Chapter 20 – Reminiscing – Again

Here's the incident about my friend Monty that I promised to tell you. This took place during a funeral procession to Fort Sam Houston National Cemetery. It happened about six months after 9/11, the atrocity which destroyed the twin towers in New York. In view of this, Fort Sam was still under tight security. After the funeral Mass we departed my parish of Saint John Berchmans, but this time I was not riding the hearse with Monty. I was riding what they call the lead car, a brand new Cadillac. This was a pricey funeral where even the minister is driven in a ritzy automobile.

When we arrived at the Fort Sam Houston main gate, my driver noticed that the hearse had stopped about twenty yards back; the battery conked out! I heard the young funeral director saying, "Oh, Lord what are we going to do now?" In my mind I was thinking: "What do you mean *we*, Kemosabe? You are the funeral director." It was a problem anyhow, as there were no more hearses available at the funeral home.

Enter Mexican ingenuity. Three cars behind the hearse was a green Suburban. The mourners in the Suburban were moved to other cars and space was made available for the casket. No problem! As we arrived at the pavilion site, I could see the honor guard sharply saluting at the new Suburban where the deceased veteran was. After I conducted my prayer graveside service, I was returned back to my church safe and sound . . . not in a hearse, but in a big, white Cadillac. From then on, when I saw Monty at church for a funeral, I reminded him: "How are you fixed for batteries?" Wise guy!

- Outside of Kress Five and Ten store in the heart of downtown Laredo was where I was a young, self-employed lemon entrepreneur at the age of eight. One block north, across from each other, were four of the top department stores in Laredo: J. C. Penney, Hachar's, Montgomery Ward, and *El Sol del Oriente*. At the time this was a busy intersection. J. C. Penney, a big store, had those huge windows nicely filled with displays of premium clothing. Outside the store were dark blue and well-designed pillars on the sidewalk, which held up a roof that shaded the sidewalk. Why do I remember all of this? I should! Yolanda, my future wife worked at Kress Department Store, a block away. I was already working in San Antonio, but during my visits to Laredo I would go pick her up at work and then go to dinner. Outside of Penney's, by those fancy blue pillars, was the spot where I proposed to her. Goodness gracious, isn't that a sentimental and romantic site for a proposal? By the way, at the time of the proposal, we were rushing to my car because the parking meter time was expiring. Yes, Laredo already had parking meters.

- Our home in Laredo was about a mile from Our Lady of Guadalupe Catholic Church. How well I remember all the noise, commotion, and disturbance after a wedding. They would tie all kinds of cans, tin containers, and God knows what else to the car bumpers, and then they would loudly honk the horns during the procession. There were times when the wedding procession would go by our house and of course Dad had his own spicy comments for the recently married. He would say: *"Que bonito; tanto ruido y tanto pedo que hacen los recien casados y a las tres semanas comienzan los rietazos."* "How cute – so much noise and crap the newlyweds make now and in three weeks the fist fights begin!" And I could hear Mom say: *"Callate, señor."* "Be quiet, man." I suppose my dad's philosophy on this matter was sometimes correct.

- María Elena, the oldest of my four sisters, and I both shared a very special, distinctive assignment. We were bilingual letter writers during our teenage years. In the spring and summer months many families in Laredo and South Texas would migrate North to harvest the fruits and vegetables in Michigan, Minnesota, Wisconsin, and other states. It was then that people came to Dad's store to talk to my sister and to me. Illiteracy was not rampant, but many people could not read or write. It was in the back porch of the house where María Elena and I sat down with our neighbors to read the letters from their relatives or friends working up north. Then they would patiently tell us what to write back to them. Dad urged us not to accept any money for this, but they insisted, and usually handed us about fifteen or twenty cents to read and write a letter. I recall that we also addressed the envelope to their relatives. By the way, at the time postage stamps were three cents each and postcards were a penny. Think about that! In high school my sister excelled in shorthand. One year she represented Martin High School in Interscholastic League competition in Austin. After high school she was employed at the Laredo Air Force Base.
- Ralph Waldo Emerson once said: *"The wise man in the storm prays to God not for safety from danger, but for deliverance from fear."* Are you scared of lightning and thunder? Who isn't? During my Navy stint at sea, I witnessed a few of the tough old salts and the bravest of sailors show an extreme fear of thunder and lightning. Psychologists tell us that some people love to watch thunder and lightning. Others are scared and develop astraphobia – a fear of thunder and lightning. In my childhood days it seemed that everyone in the house was scared during a storm. Me too! I remember well that my Aunt Rosa would cover all mirrors in the house with bed sheets. Now, what kind of

witchcraft is that? Is that going to help matters? Another thing Aunt Rosa did was that during those ugly electrical storms she would pray a lot. Every time the lightning flashed and the thunder crashed all around, my aunt would say: *"Jesús, María y José"* or "Jesus, Mary and Joseph." My math tells me that if there were 26 lightning flashes and 26 thunder crashes in the storm, then my aunt Rosa repeated: *"Jesús, María y José,"* fifty-two times. Incredible!

- Whenever I go to Laredo, I enjoy visiting with my younger brother Beto, my sister-in-law Rosie, and my nephew Danny. In the evening, Beto and I sit outside in the patio where we wet our whistles with a cold sarsaparilla and smoke expensive Havana cigars, as we reminisce and dig up the past. How's that for a cool evening in Laredo? Some times my other nephew and police officer Betito comes over, and there is a small barbeque. Beto is quite a guitar player and at times he will sing us a song or two. I must say that my brother is also a good gardener, as he keeps his backyard well manicured and clean. He cares for a number of beautiful flowers and plants and I wonder sometimes how he can keep a tidy well-kept garden during the hot days in Laredo. Thank you, brother Beto, for the wonderful evenings I have enjoyed in your patio.

- As you have already read, I have a flood of memories about Dad. Some years ago I went to one of the malls here in San Antonio – something that I seldom do. I saw a huge remodeled gym and exercise area in the mall, which really caught my eye. It was an immense gym with a multitude of equipment like treadmills, incline trainers, weights, Nordic tracks, dumbbells, and other silly and expensive apparatus that I don't have any use for. People will waste their money on these things and I say – more power to them. My dad never saw these dumb contraptions, but I believe he would had said something like this: *"Mi hijo, para un buen ejercicio, mejor agarra el rastrío y el azadón y hasle la lucha al trompío, en lugar de andar de payaso con esas maquinas."* "My son, for a good exercise grab the hoe and the rake and tackle the *trompío* instead of clowning around with those machines." The *trompío* is a wild thorny weed and a menace to many flower gardens in Laredo. This then, would be my dad's abbreviated opinion on the exercise machines.

• Laredo is remembered on the Strait of Juan de Fuca. Where and what is the Strait of Juan de Fuca? In the northwest part of our country it is an arm of the sea or an inlet of water from the Pacific Ocean that forms the international boundary between the United States and Canada. The strait is over 105 miles long and about 20 miles wide. There is an international vehicle ferry that crosses the strait from Port Angeles, Washington, to beautiful Victoria, British Columbia, Canada. This huge ferry carries more than 150 vehicles and over 1,000 passengers. In September 1997, I played golf at the scenic Gorge Vale golf course in Victoria. The following day as I returned to Port Angeles aboard the ferry, I met quite an articulate and free-spoken man. He was the U.S. Immigration Service supervisor for the area, and he was conducting the customary inspections aboard the ferry on all cars coming to the U.S. When he got to my car he asked for identification and also to open the car trunk. After he saw my driver's license and noticed my San Antonio address, he launched an intensive conversation. He told me that years ago, he was stationed as an immigration officer in El Paso, Laredo, and Los Ébanos, Texas. We talked about the Laredo area, the Casablanca golf course, (obviously, he saw my golf clubs in the trunk) as he proceeded to tell me his adventures as a young man in the border city. In the lengthy conversation we covered a number of subjects. Then over the ferry loudspeaker he was told to hurry up with his inspections. He was actually behind on his inspection duties and the ferry was nearing Port Angeles. In a cool way he told me: "I am the boss here, what's the rush, there is no problem. Besides, I'll retire in two months." As I viewed the scenic waters of the Strait, I heard him say: "This is a beautiful day. People rush and worry too much. So tell me, what else is new in good ole Laredo, Texas?"

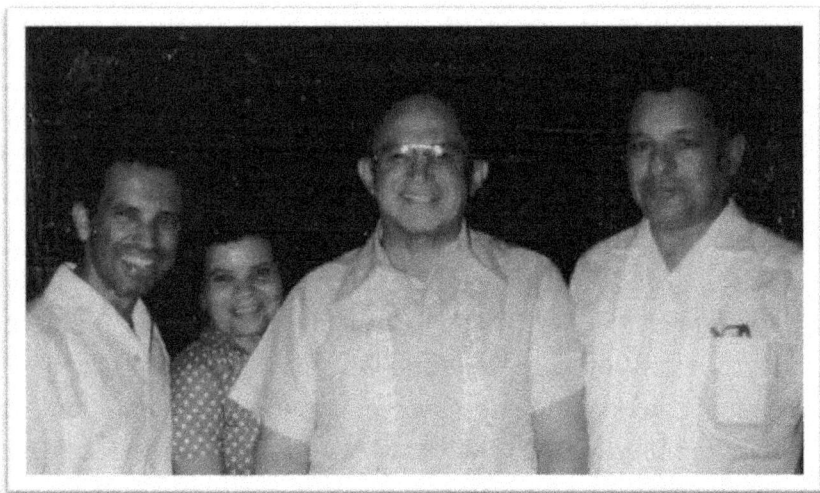

Fr. David García, my wife, Archbishop Flores, and myself.

Chapter 21 – Ordained a Deacon

"Are you resolved to discharge the office of Deacon with humility and love in order to assist the bishops and to serve the people of God?" – Roman Pontifical

On the 3rd day of November 1983, almost three years before my retirement from Federal Service, I was accepted into the Permanent Diaconate program of the Archdiocese of San Antonio. My wife and children, my pastor and church community were pleased and delighted. As I reflected and looked forward to my studies that would lead to a lifetime commitment of ordained service to God, I felt such a powerful expression of God's love for me. I felt his eternal love as an all loving Father and I suppose the apostle Saint John said it best: *"For God is love."* Now, at my age I would get back into the old school grind of homework, studying, and burning the midnight oil. I calculated that it would not be easy.

About twenty-four candidates formed the deacon class of 1987, and we came from different parishes and rural areas of the Archdiocese. During the course of our formation, some students left the program and others were booted out. Most of the new class was not that old, but we were not young, either. Some of us walked a little slower; our eyes and hearing were not what they once were. Perhaps a few of us thought we were over the hill but you know what, there was the desire and prayerful hope that we would do well in our vocation and be ordained ministers and servants of God. In September of 1985, we completed the first step to ordination, as we were installed in the Ministry of Reader by Auxiliary Bishop Bernard Popp. This means that we now preach the gospel, the good news of Christ to those who do not know it, and to give the children and adults instruction in the faith. In November of 1986, we completed our second and final step. In ceremonies at Assumption Seminary chapel, Archbishop Patrick Flores installed us in the Ministry of Acolyte. This was a beautiful and sacred ceremony where the Archbishop told us that as we share the Eucharist with our brothers and sisters, we become one body with them. He told us to have a genuine love for the body of Christ, and to pattern our lives on the commandment the Lord gave his apostles at the Last Supper: "Love one another as I have loved you."

The months and years of our Deacon formation went fast and soon it would be Ordination Day. How did we do it? Many people are not really aware of the effort and work that a deacon candidate must endure. It is not easy, as you have to support and take care of a family. Some candidates had two jobs and some, like me, were also attending college night classes. Many professors really loaded us with homework. One I have in mind is Dr. Barbara Herlihy, Professor of Holy Scripture, who really poured it on the old-timers with homework. As a matter of fact, Mrs. Herlihy had an affectionate title given by someone in the class. She was known as Barbara "Homework by the Pound" Herlihy. I often wonder who gave her that appropriate nickname. Ask me and I'll gladly tell you. Anyway, of all the teachers, professors, and counselors I had during my deacon formation studies, Dr. Herlihy stands out as distinguished. She was a true professional and my best teacher as she enriched my love for the Scriptures. What I learned from her eventually helped me later when I taught English and Spanish Bible classes in my parish for more than fifteen years.

Dr. Barbara Herlihy attended my first Mass and my first homily that I preached as an ordained deacon in my parish of Saint John Berchmans. This was a special day for me and I remember it so well. It was the 21st of June 1987, the Feast of Corpus Christi, or the

Solemnity of the most Holy Body and Blood of Christ. I introduced Barbara to my congregation during the Mass as a courageous and gallant lady for putting up with the veterans and old-timers of the class of '87. God bless you, Barbara . . . thank you for showing me the truth and the beauty of the Bible. *"Your word is a lamp to my feet and a light for my path."* (Psalm 119:105) I sincerely believed that all the subjects and the curriculum in my deacon formation were beneficial and applicable for our ministry. The teachers and professors were knowledgeable in their respective subjects, which were many. Some of these subjects were: social ethics, Christology, pastoral counseling, the sacraments, moral theology, homiletics, canon law, and marriage, plus some others. Without any doubt, my favorite subjects were sacred scripture and church history.

On June 7, 1987, on the Feast of Pentecost, I was promoted and conferred in the Holy Order of Deacon by Archbishop Patrick F. Flores, of the Archdiocese of San Antonio. There were seventeen of us (the Class of '87) who were ordained Deacons at Saint Matthews Church in San Antonio, where my family, friends, and many of my parishioners were present for the ceremony. My pastor of Saint John Berchmans church, Father Frank Vanhee, CICM, was also present to receive from the Archbishop the *pagella* or the official duties and ministries granted to me. My official assignment from the Archbishop was to be Deacon to my parish of Saint John Berchmans. I received another blessing from the good Lord as I would begin my Diaconal ministries under a devout and a caring priest. Soon, he gave me an open mandate and authorization to perform such ministries and duties according to my available time. In no time at all I had a complete schedule of assignments: assisting at the altar during Sunday Masses, preaching, teaching scripture classes, hospital visits, and the three important duties that we Deacons call in our trade: "We hatch 'em, we match 'em, and we dispatch 'em,'" meaning that we perform baptisms, marriages, and funerals.

It is important for me to mention and give credit to the CICM priests. Who were they? It stands for *Congregatio Immaculati Cordis Marie*, or the Congregation of the Immaculate Heart of Mary. It is a Catholic missionary order of priests and brothers founded in Belgium in 1862. Today CICM is present in Singapore, China, the Philippines, Africa, Haiti, Guatemala, Mexico, Brazil, and the U.S. In 2010, my parish, Saint John Berchmans, celebrated its 100th anniversary and it has been staffed by CICM until 1992. That year they were replaced by Diocesan priests. As of this year, I have been in my parish for 54 years and I am so blessed to have ministered and worked together with many tireless and unselfish CICM priests. Among them were Fathers Michael Cattaert, William Lievens, Paul Newhouse, Theo Clerx, Frank Vanhee, José Michels, Bart Flaat, David Perez, Mario Vanderwolk, Roger Newton, Clement DeMeersman, and Albert VanNuffelen. After the CICM departure, the last four Diocesan priests I worked with were Eddie Bernal, Jim Hynes, Carlos Velasquez, and Rudy Carrola.

As stated before, the orders from my boss Archbishop Flores on ordination were that I would be assigned Deacon duties at Saint John Berchmans. However, three months later, on September 25, 1987, I received a letter signed by the Archbishop giving me additional duties in the Office of the Director of Deacons. Father Jack O'Donoghue, Director of Deacons, furnished me with my new assignments and tasks. The duties consisted of administering the 30-minute taped interviews for the new deacon candidates, the wife and deacon counseling at home for potential deacons, some administrative chores in the Diaconate office, and assisting in teaching homiletics for the new deacon candidates here in San Antonio and Uvalde, Texas. Once or twice a month I would travel with Deacon John Landez to teach homiletics in Uvalde. This class consisted of students from Eagle Pass, Del Río, Uvalde, Batesville, Kerrville, and Brackettville. These homiletic classes in San Antonio and Uvalde lasted for almost eleven years.

My Deacon schedule was sufficient and satisfactory now. With my parish duties and my seminary work with the deacon candidates and teaching, I still found time for my work at home. Of course, as stated in Diaconate rubrics, my wife and home came first. We traveled intensively to visit our two daughters in North Texas. We traveled to Laredo to see our families, and to California and Las Vegas to see my sisters. Added to that were our long trips to different parts of the country to attend my Navy reunions. Naturally, I won't forget the many trips around Texas that we traveled together for me to play in golf tournaments.

On the Feast of Pentecost, the 27th of May 2012, my parish of Saint John Berchmans honored me with a luncheon at the school cafeteria on my 25th anniversary as an ordained Deacon. I assisted at the 10:00 a.m. Mass and preached my last homily. My family was there from Dallas, Fort Worth, Houston, and Laredo, and also from Turlock, California, and Reno, Nevada. Actually, one never retires from serving the Lord, but my Diaconal duties as Servant of the Lord in Saint John Berchmans ended on this beautiful Sunday of Pentecost.

As a personal tribute to my parish, I sincerely offer my praise and accolades to Saint John Berchmans church. In my 53 years of service to this parish I worked with so many good and faithful parishioners. Additionally, we had at the time some magnificent leaders that made me so proud of their dedication for the well-being of the church community. Through these years Saint John Berchmans was definitely a parish of growth and collaboration. Some of my parish duties before ordination included President of the Holy Name Society, Chairman of the Finance Committee, Member of the School Board, and Men's Club Treasurer. Nonetheless, and not showing any favoritism, it was the Catholic education of the youth that was my fond and devoted ministry. It was the CCD (Confraternity of Christian Doctrine) that was very dear to me. Father Bill Lievens, Deacon Bill Schiebel, Sister Paula Billiet, and I were the leaders of this program. For fourteen years I labored with this project – nine as an 11th grade teacher, three as a vice-principal, and two as principal of the High School of Religion. At the time we had 1,000 students in the program and I had over 330 in High School. In the early 1970's the Vatican selected Saint John Berchmans as the best and Number One CCD School in the United States. Soon after this, the story of our successful CCD School appeared in a Catholic national weekly newspaper. Parishes from different parts of the country wrote to us to find out just how we did it. They would ask: "What are you teaching, what is your curriculum, how about your teachers, just what makes you great?" In view of this, we prepared a small booklet with our guidelines, responsibilities, and directions on how we managed our CCD school in Saint John Berchmans. This booklet was then mailed to parishes around the country that wanted to know about our excellent program.

There was a pastor from an Ohio parish that wrote saying: "You have a booming and a successful CCD program at Saint John Berchmans in San Antonio – just how in God's name did you do it?" Quickly I wrote him back to tell him that he answered his own question because it was in God's name that we did it. We put God first, next the parents, then the children, and then the teachers and staff. It was the parents who made the effort to send their kids to CCD school. It was the parents who were hungry for a firm and a good Christian education for their children.

"It was not you who chose me, but I who chose you and appointed you to go and bear fruit that will remain." (John 15: 16)

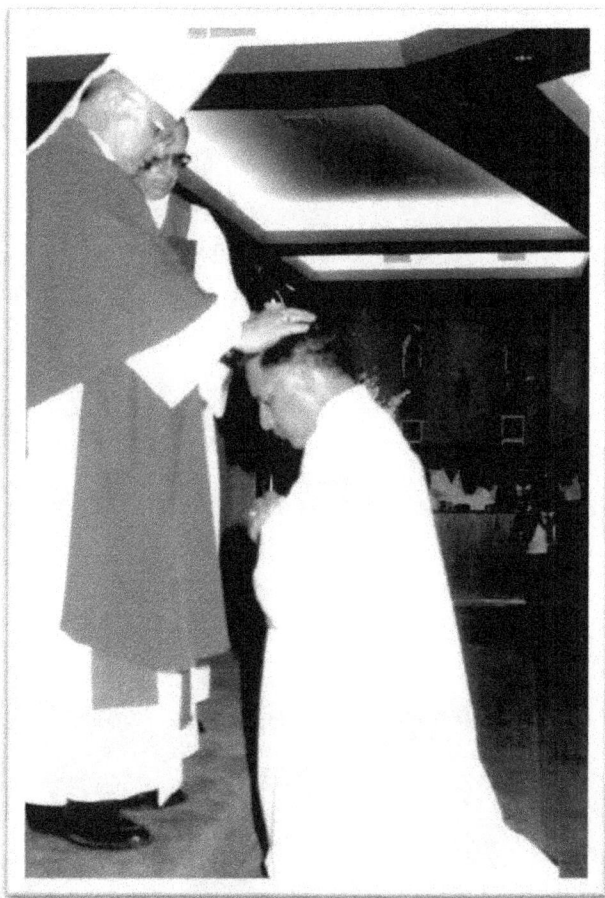

June 1987 – My deacon ordination by Archbishop Patrick Flores of the Archdiocese of San Antonio. "The laying of hands – a deacon forever."

CICM priests and deacons at my ordination mass, 1987

Ordination Day 1987; Archbishop Flores hands me my assignment.

Deacon ordination day, with my wife Yolanda.

As principal of St. John Berchman's CCD High School of Religion, I'm addressing the student body before introducing Congressman Henry B. Gonzalez (seated).

Chapter 22 – Pope John Paul II Visits San Antonio

On the 13th of September, 1987, San Antonio was honored and blessed with the presence of a great man – the leader of the Catholic Church, the successor of Saint Peter and soon to be saint, Pope John Paul II. The morning after his arrival at Kelly AFB, his motorcade took him to a 250-acre site in Westover Hills, where the pontifical mass was celebrated. It was history in the making; never before in San Antonio or Texas had there been so many people assembled for a single event. There were 350,000 people attending the service, which was seen on television around the world. There were 5,000 ushers and 3,000 eucharistic ministers, and choir members came from all over the Lone Star State to assist in the liturgy. Hundreds of priests and deacons assisted in the service, as well as 35 bishops from all over the country, and from Mexico and Canada. Also in attendance were more than 300 ecumenical leaders from all faiths, denominations, and religious communities. People came from all over the United States. Catholic churches in Laredo and other border towns organized tours and special busses for the long trip to San Antonio to see Pope John Paul and be a part of the historic mass.

I was honored and blessed to have a part in it also, to serve as Eucharistic minister for the mass. Also serving from my parish was our pastor, Fr. Frank VanHee, the last of our CICM priests, and my good friend Deacon Librado Cena, a decorated hero of the Koren War. It was Deacon Cena who drove us to the Westover Hills – and it took us a while to walk from the parking lot to the altar area. I figured it was about a mile or more. The three of us along with other priests and deacons had choice seats. We were just two rows from the main altar. The mass was supposed to start at 11 a.m., but by that time it was already as hot and humid as had been predicted. Days before, the newspapers and television stations had been warning San

Antonians to be careful of the extreme hot weather conditions they were anticipating for the mass. When communion time arrived, an usher took us blocks away where we were to distribute the Eucharist to the people. As I walked to that area, I could see many places offering cold water. All over the area there were medical services available, along with fire and police protection.

Today's Catholic, the diocesan newspaper reported the following: *"The Mass went well. Smashingly good. And, out of a crowd of a third-of-a-million people, there were surprisingly few health problems. Two people had strokes, two babies were delivered, and eight people needed to be hospitalized."*

Each eucharistic minister at the mass was given a *ciborium*, or container for the sacred hosts. This ceramic bowl could hold up to 300 hosts. After the service, this container was presented to us as a memento or keepsake. I still have this container and each time I look at it, I am reminded of that beautiful, warm, historic day when I saw the Pope, and where I served as communion minister – and yes, it was a 'one in a lifetime' experience. There were deacons from my ordination class who served as communion ministers along with hundreds of others from all over the state.

It was a great joy to see Deacon John Landez, of St. Leo's parish, serve alongside Pope John Paul at the altar. Deacon Landez was selected from among all the other deacons in Texas to be the Deacon of the Table, and to assist the pope during mass. What an honor and what a responsibility! Deacon Landez was a man of great humility and patience. For about eleven years I assisted him in teaching homiletics to the new candidates at the seminary, and then for some years in Uvalde.

After knowing that the Pope would officially visit Texas, Archbishop Patrick Flores selected Father (now Monsignor) Lawrence Steubben to be *'El Jefe'* or the statewide coordinator for the papal visit. And what an outstanding job he did in the organizing and management of that huge project. After the visit, Monsignor

Steubben summarized his efforts and his feelings by saying that Pope John Paul II was the most significant leader of the Church in the last sixteen years, and probably a saint. And you know what, Monsignor Steubben – you were right, because very soon, Pope John Paul II will be canonized as a saint of the Catholic Church.

Here's a note of interest about Monsignor Steubben: I usually saw him in the chancery or at the seminary, especially in the SUB, the Student Union Building, where I was teaching. Days and weeks before the annual Irish Open – a very popular golf tournament for priests and deacons – he would always tell me, "I want you to do some butt-kicking in the golf tournament and keep those priests and deacons humble!" However, through the years, I never once asked him, "Who is going to keep *me* humble?"

Chapter 23 – What is a Blessing?

In South Texas a blessing is something meaningful and significant. For most families a blessing is considered very important to parents and children. It could be a ritual blessing, a formal blessing, or simply the sign of the cross. Keep in mind that a blessing is an expression of your faith, and through the blessing a person may receive protection, peace, and favors from God. My dad considered a blessing as something effective and very powerful.

First, let me clearly specify here that a blessing is not limited to a bishop, priest, a deacon, or any minister. Many parents bless their children and a person will bless each other with a simple phrase like: *"Dios te bendiga,"* or *"Valla con Dios,"* – *"God bless you,"* or *"God be with you."* Parents will bless their sons and daughters who are getting married or departing on a trip. Traditionally, a dying parent would bless their children. On a sad note, many of these religious customs and traditions like the blessing are being forgotten. Much of the younger generation (in some cases, not only the young) openly will state that all of this is antiquated and obsolete. Some say that all of these rituals are not needed in our modern age of science and computers. Not true.

How well I remember all the blessings that I received from my dad. Did I need them that bad? Of course I did! In my younger days, upon my departures from my home in Laredo to San Antonio, Dad would always bless me before getting in the car. As I left the house and drove north on San Darío Avenue, I could still see Dad blessing me with the sign of the cross. Have you ever heard of a long-distance blessing? Once a week my sister Carmen was given a blessing by phone from Dad. At about 10:00 a.m. every Saturday morning

(Laredo time) Carmen called home from California. At the end of the lengthy conversation she wanted my dad's blessing over the phone.

In my parish, the parents of the child being baptized had to attend instruction classes. Before I baptized the child I would encourage the parents to bless the child every night and morning. I have always said that a parent's blessing on a child really packs a powerful spiritual punch. I urge you to get in a daily habit of blessing your son, daughter, and everyone in the family. From the beginning until the end of time, all of God's work is a blessing. From the very beginning our creator God blessed every living being, especially man and woman. A blessing really means that God looks with favor upon all persons and things.

Priests and Deacons are asked to bless children and adults. Other blessings are for a person going on a trip, or going to the hospital. An important item for families is the blessing of a home. Cars, religious articles, rosaries, statues, and medals can be blessed also. A blessing is an expression of faith and belief in God's love and protection.

Chapter 24 – The Journey

"There is an appointed time for everything, and a time for every affair under the heavens. A time to be born, and a time to die. A time to kill and a time to heal; a time to weep and a time to laugh; a time to mourn and a time to dance. A time to love and a time to hate; a time of war and a time of peace. – Ecclesiastes 3: 1-8

After teaching Holy Scripture for more than fifteen years in my parish and two years in Poteet, Texas, I still affirm that Ecclesiastes is one of my favorite books in the Bible. According to both Jewish and Christian traditions, King Solomon is the author of this book. Ecclesiastes is concerned with the purpose and value of human life. It deals primarily with man looking for happiness on this earth without ever finding it. But this important book also brings to mind an impressive truth and doctrine that I learned from my dad.

One time Dad took me to a wake or a vigil service. I had never seen a dead person before. My Uncle Juan who lived just outside of the city had died. Years ago, many people had an all-night vigil in their homes. The body of the deceased was kept at home so there was a Rosary and an all-night prayer service there. That evening, as we neared my uncle's house I could hear loud music. It was really loud and boisterous with accordion and drums; real cantina music. The little ranch nearby apparently was having some kind of celebration. I asked Dad why all the noise and why not show respect for the dead?

Here's the answer: "First, maybe they don't know of the dead person, or maybe they could care less. Right now it is their time for enjoyment. Someday they will be mourning and we will be celebrating. This is how life goes and there is a time for everything." Isn't this the same logic from King Solomon? Thus, during our journey on earth there is an appointed time for everything . . . including the end of that journey.

Not all of us have been blessed with a good journey here on this earth. But whether it is good or bad, someday the journey will finish. How about your journey; has it been fruitful and productive? For many of us the journey has not been a walk in the park – a journey of wine and roses. This world has seldom been a peaceful or tranquil place to live. As I mentioned before, we live in a world of violence, hate, animosity, crime, jealousy, revenge, envy, and greed. We do not live in a Utopia or the Celestial City. Do you know what a "speed bump" is? They are placed on the streets to slow us down and to ensure our safety and the safety of others. To me, a speed bump can really be annoying, but in our life's journey there are many speed bumps. These can be bumps in our married life, health problems, our financial problems, or our spiritual problems.

There is not a single person in the world that has not traveled over speed bumps. In my journey I have wandered, traveled, and navigated through many of those speed bumps of life. My journey – and you have read most of it now – has been a road of many bumps, almost like a roller coaster ride. I believe God puts you through all of this just to show what's in you. The last three years that my wife lived on this earth was a painful speed bump in my life. The doctor told me that in addition to a stroke which she had suffered, she now had the early symptoms of Parkinson's disease, a disorder of the central nervous system. I know Ernesto Garza, my doctor, very well. As a deacon candidate, Dr. Garza was one of my students when I was teaching homiletics at the seminary. In view of this, he was candid with me in addressing my wife's health. With all my faith and trust in God I took care of her for nearly three years. God's graces continued for me as I was blessed and fortunate that my deacon friend and doctor would personally come to the house to examine my wife. Finally, about two-

and-half years later her health worsened and a nursing home was mandatory.

On Saturday, the 25th of November of the year 2000, two days after Thanksgiving Day, my wife Yolanda departed from this life, bound for God's kingdom. My wife of 43 years, my high school sweetheart, and that little girl I knew since the first grade was now in the loving arms of her Creator. I really felt the speed bumps now; this was the worst knock-down punch in my journey. As painful and difficult as it was, my happiness and my joys were exhausting and draining. But in the deep recess of my mind I could hear His voice, loud and clear: *"I will never forsake you, I will never abandon you."* (Hebrews 13: 5) God in his mercy and his love touched my life. As tough as it was, my journey must continue. *"Fiat voluntas tua." "Thy will be done."*

My wife was well-liked in our parish of Saint John Berchmans. At one time she was a eucharistic minister and a fourth grade CCD teacher. This brings up one dear memory; the Rosary for my wife was held in the church and many people attended. The big boss, Archbishop Patrick Flores, was there. The director of deacons, priests, and many of my brother deacons also attended. My family and I were sitting in the first pew, next to the sanctuary. My daughter Patty had already told Ryan, my ten-year-old grandson, to stand up when people came to offer their condolences. Immediately after the rosary was over, Ryan came up to me and said, "Grandma must have been well-liked in this church because I received handshakes from so many people that I had to be standing up over and over again. Golly, Grandpa, I was getting tired!"

"Sic Gloria transit mundi." – "The glory of the world passes."

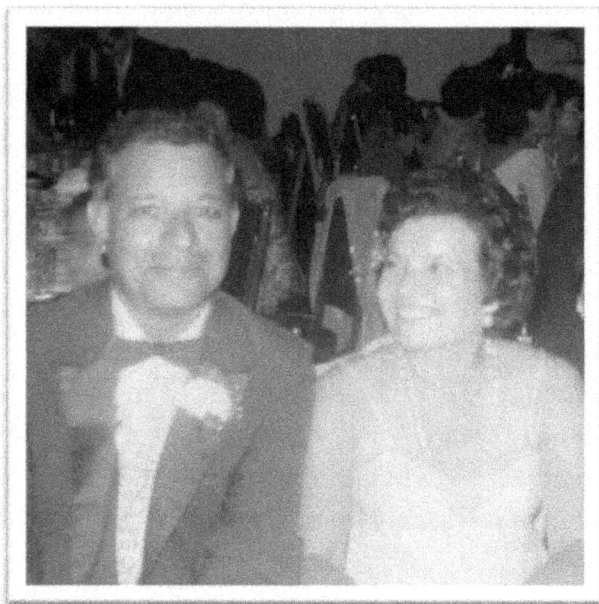

October, 1982 – Our 25th wedding anniversary.

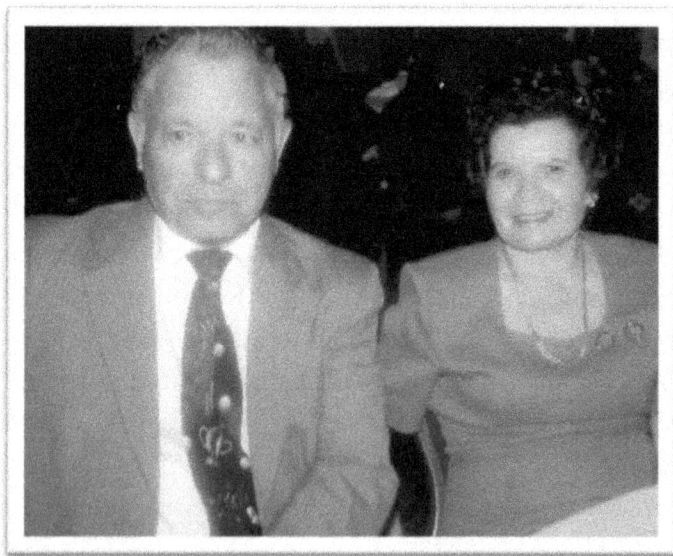

My wife Yolanda and I at the USS Antietam reunion, 1996, in Hagerstown, Maryland.

Chapter 25 – The Surrender

"Lord, you have made us for yourself, and our hearts are restless until they rest in You." Saint Augustine of Hippo

Three persons, or should I say three saints, come to mind as I write about the surrender. First, my great hero, Saint Paul of Tarsus, then Saint Augustine of Hippo, and finally Saint Ignatius Loyola. But to what did they surrender and just what is a surrender? To surrender is to say that you are defeated – to throw in the towel or wave the white flag. It is to tell your opponent that he has won and the fighting is over. Another definition of surrender is to relinquish possession or control of something.

When we surrender to God we are plainly admitting and recognizing that whether we like it not, all that we are and all that we own actually belongs to Him, who is the giver of all things. By surrendering to God we are admitting that He is in control of everything; that includes our bodies, our mind, our health, our speech, our savings account, our plans, our goals . . . everything. Even our next breath comes from Him. Our very existence is a divine gift from Him. When we surrender to God we let go of whatever has been holding us back from the best that God has for our lives. It is a complete and total giving of us to Him. *"Una entrega completa a Él."*

Do you think it's an easy thing to surrender? Absolutely not! The great saints who were great sinners also, had problems with this. Some, like us, were so much attached to the world and to the good and bad of it alike. But the saints knew that because God is our creator He deserves our best. He gave us His best and that is Himself. He opened his arms on the cross and died for us, because He loved us. Remember that we are his sheep, He is the Shepherd; we are his servants, He is the Master; we are the clay, He is the Potter; we are his creation, He is the Creator. He is our Redeemer, Messiah, and Savior. Shouldn't we surrender to Him then? It is to him that some day you and I will have to render an account of ourselves. *"Every one of us will have to give an account of himself before God."* (Romans 14: 12) On that day we shall face him by ourselves, without the best attorneys to defend us. When we face the Almighty, it will a one-on-one – *un mano a mano.*

The three saints mentioned above made a complete surrender to their master. It was a total conversion or a change. I call it an improvement or a transformation – a change from the darkness to the light. Because of that great love for their master, the saints relinquished all. The first act of being a good Christian is to surrender. Saint Ignatius was a soldier and wanted to be a military leader. After being seriously wounded in the battle of Pamplona, he underwent a spiritual conversion while in recovery. He was a million miles from the will of God. After recuperating, God had something on the agenda for him. Almighty God has worked a purpose for you and me here below. He has things for us – not the things that we want. He has a plan for you and me. *"For I know well the plans I have in mind for you, says the Lord, plans for your welfare, plans to give you a future full of hope."* (Jeremiah 29: 11-12) The surrender to God in the journey is worth it. It was worth and beneficial for Ignatius. It has been great and beneficial for me and so will it be for you.

Almighty God has been so good and generous to us. Just consider all the benefits and blessings He has given us. Jesus his Son didn't have to leave the beauty and the splendor of heaven to come to this troubled world. He didn't, but He loved us and one of the most powerful passages in the Bible tells us just how much He loved us: *"For God so loved the world that He gave his only son, so that everyone who believes in him might not perish but might have eternal life."* (John 3: 16) Now, that is love; that is real love. Who else has done that for us? No one! Just think, Jesus was enjoying the beauty of heaven and he came to this earth to be beaten, battered, and bruised, and then crucified. Yes, he carried all my sins and your sins to the cross and then he died. He loved us. Isn't this worth a surrender to Him?

Jesus said: *"Whoever wishes to come after me must deny himself, take up his cross and follow me."* (Matthew 16: 24) Don't forget that during our journey you and I must carry many crosses. Some of you are feeling the weight of those heavy crosses right now. When we surrender to God, the crosses will still be there. In my daily prayers I always ask the Lord not to stop sending me any more crosses – the crosses will be with us forever. What I ask in my prayers is for the Lord to give me strength and strong shoulders to carry any cross he might send me. In one of my Christology classes in the seminary one deacon candidate asked the question: "How long will I have to carry crosses?" The professor without any hesitation said: "Twenty-three seconds after you are buried you will stop carrying crosses." The prof was overestimating it a bit, but he made his point very clear.

In our journey the crosses you and I will have to carry could be sickness, death of a loved one, marriage problems, loneliness, economic failures, depression – the list goes on. Many times there is so much hurt and pain as we bear the crosses. But you know what? Christ knows very well the weight of those crosses we carry daily and He is filled with compassion for our sufferings and our sorrows. As I said before, Jesus carried his cross – for you and for me – all the way to Calvary. And through that horrible death and then his glorious resurrection He won our salvation for us. How blessed we are! So it is the cross, an instrument of torture and death that becomes for us Christians the symbol of hope and refuge. And when the crosses get heavy, when there is suffering in our lives, when we are up to our ears with problems, when we barely see the light at the end of the tunnel, Christ wants to help us carry our crosses and He already promised that He will lighten our burdens and our sorrows. On one occasion He said: *"Come to me, all you who labor and are burdened, and I will give you rest."* (Matthew 11: 28)

To sum it all up, the surrender is worth it.

Chapter 26 – A Time for Thanksgiving

"Give thanks to Him; bless His name, for He is good. – Psalm 100:4

During my childhood days in Laredo, it was a requirement that I should be grateful and offer thanksgiving to our Creator for the food that I was about to partake. The effects of the Great Depression could still be felt, but my mother always insisted that no matter how meager and scarce our nutrition was, God deserved our thanks for every meal. This was a must. In the many years of teaching scripture in my parish, one of the most popular lessons for my adult class was the one on prayer. What is prayer? Many Christians agree that prayer is talking with God. Prayer means to communicate with God, and the word "with" is the clue. Prayer is talking <u>with</u> God and not just to God. More than this, Christian prayer is a conversation with the supreme King of the universe. I would teach my class to pray in this order:

<u>Adoration</u> – This should be first. Almighty God before anyone else deserves all the praise, honor, and glory. He is our heavenly Father and Creator of heaven and earth. He is our Lord and King. He is the big boss – He is *número uno*.

<u>Forgiveness</u> – We ask his forgiveness for the many times we have offended Him, and for the many times we have failed Him. Saint Paul tells us that, "All have sinned and come short of the glory of God." Therefore, in all humility we should repent and ask forgiveness of God.

<u>Thanksgiving</u> – We owe God so many thanks as He has given us so much. He has given us this day, the gift of life, our health, our job, and our food. He has given us his Son, Jesus Christ. He gives us our daily bread plus many other graces, benefits, and blessings.

<u>Petition</u> – (Asking) Jesus tell us to ask and we shall receive. Many times we use this petition so liberal . . . Lord, give me this and that . . . I want a new car, I want, I want a new house, I want good numbers for the lottery – gimme, gimme. God doesn't give you what you want; He gives you what you need. There are times that in our prayers we put Petition before Adoration. Am I correct?

My journey has been one full-bloom and loaded with Thanksgiving. I am thankful and appreciative to the people that supported me in my ministry. I begin with thanking my Master first. I thank him for my family in Laredo and other parts of the country. Thank you, Lord, for my wife and children. I thank God for my profession of 35 years in Federal service. I thank God for my college education, my seminary training, and for my military service. Thanks, Lord, for all my relatives and all my dear friends. Every day I offer thanks to God for the protection he gave me as I traveled the fifty states of America, in Canada, Mexico, and countries in the Pacific. Many generous and good people have blessed me in my journey. I am grateful to all of them. They have prayed for me and they have inspired me, and they have touched my life. They stood behind me in thick and thin.

Once again I thank my parents who were certainly the first teachers in my first seminary – my home. These are the words of Archbishop Flores from some of the talks that he gave us as deacon candidates. He stressed that the home is the first seminary, where as a child you not only have the best teachers, but the best counselors, instructors, and advisors – your parents. It is not the school, the Boy Scouts, the church, or the government; it is your parents. Your first training begins at home. It is the seminary at home where the first seed is planted, nourished, and allowed to grow. Again I must say that during my childhood years in Laredo, my parents were poor and they were in need. However, I don't hold poverty against my parents; in the midst of that poverty they were together with each other and together with us. Even then as a child I could feel that we needed nothing else because we had the love and care of a righteous mother and father. In the few years that I was doing counseling I saw children that lived in fancy, beautiful homes, who had all the material things available, but no parental love. All those beautiful things can never make up for the love and concern of a mother and father. Like many parents, Mom and Dad promised to remain faithful to God and to each other in sickness and in health, in poverty, in good times, and in bad times. May there be love, peace, and harmony in every family, and may God always be present to bless abundantly the parents and children.

As I near the finish line in my journey I thank my Creator, but I am also grateful and thankful to all of you. To finish, I will close with a beautiful story about heaven. A few years ago, the subject of the Bible lesson that I was teaching was Heaven. *"He will wipe every tear from your eyes, and there shall be no more death, or mourning, wailing or pain."* (Revelation 21: 4) Isn't that wonderful? God promised that to us. Just think no more pain, no more sickness, no more jealousy or envy. We shall be like God in Heaven – we will be changed. Just imagine, no more diets, calorie counting, or wrinkles. In Heaven we will never get old. We will see God face to face, and we will possess and enjoy God's company forever. Isn't that nice? My class discussed and compared all notes and observations about the Celestial City. Finally, I asked the class of about 28 men and women this one question, "How many of you want to go to Heaven?" Everyone raised hands. Perfect! After that, I asked them: "How many of you want to go to Heaven tomorrow?" There was a complete silence in the classroom – no noise – you could hear a pin drop. Ave María, everything came to a screeching halt. Finally, one lady speaking in a gentle and mild voice told me: "Deacon Díaz, I can't go to Heaven tomorrow, I have to go to the mall." Another lady very humbly said: "I can't go to Heaven tomorrow, I will miss my *novelas*." (Soap operas) Finally, to my dear English Bible class in Saint John Berchmans I remind you that Heaven is waiting for us. I'll see you there – I hope!

Chapter 27 – Final Observations

Psalm 90 in the Bible gives us a factual and legitimate account of our old age. This beautiful Psalm tells us; *"Our life is over like a sigh. Our life span is seventy years or eighty for those who are strong. And most of these are emptiness and pain. They pass swiftly and we are gone. Make us know the shortness of our life."*

This Bible passage always amazes me. It brings up the life of my dad on this earth. He lived to be past 100 years old, so what can you say – did he beat the odds? Dad had quite a sense of humor. On one occasion an old friend asked him, "Mr. Díaz, you have lived a long life, did you ever have enemies?" Right off the bat, Dad replied: "Yes, I had enemies and I outlived them all." My journey and your journey will come to an end someday. We should be ready! The Psalmist also tells us something powerful in Psalm 90. He said: *"Make us know the shortness of our lives that we may gain wisdom of heart."* In our journey one should love, obey, and serve God. With that said, I believe one should also enjoy life. Enjoy life because life has an expiration date. Aboard ship we learned this honest statistic: "One out of one dies, so enjoy life." How truthful is that? Enjoy life . . . and if this morning you didn't see your name in the obituary column of your newspaper, give thanks and rejoice.

My advice: "Enjoy life at a young age, enjoy life at a middle age, and *wow*, enjoy life (if you can) in old age." What is wrong with that? Do you know that as we grow older we are worth a fortune? Of course we are! We have silver in our hair, gold in our teeth, stones in our kidneys, lead in our feet, and gas in our stomachs. Is that worth a fortune or not? Nowadays some of us walk a little slower and our eyes and hearing are not what they once were. However, some of us remember when gasoline was 21 cents a gallon, when milk and ice was delivered to your house, and when cars were started with a crank. Remember those days? I know you do.

Once in a while I kid around and wisecrack about our old age with my brother Gonzalo from Houston. For example he might say, "Brother, you are so old that you get winded playing chess." I retaliate by saying: "Brother, you are so old you can't get the rocking chair started." And we carry on forever. "You are so old – a fortune teller reads your face instead of your hands." "You are so old you sink your teeth into a taco and they stay there." Our life is over like a sigh. Good luck in your journey, my friends. Enjoy the speed bumps and the roller coaster. Remember, there is one thing that God CANNOT do – He cannot stop loving you.

"Ad majorem dei Gloria."

Chapter 28 – *Hasta La Vista*

In a final tribute to my hometown I will say this: In 1949, when I left to join the Navy, Laredo had a population of about 58,000. Since then the Gateway City has experienced a considerable growth, not only in population but in commerce, business, and technology. With its current population soon to reach a quarter of a million, my prediction is (and I am not a demographer) that in a few years Laredo will surpass Corpus Christi and Plano, Texas. Presently, Laredo ranks as the 10th largest city in the state. No longer is Laredo that sleepy hamlet in South Texas, that one-horse town where nothing could possibly happen. Laredo is now a thriving metropolis and with the Eagle Ford shale boom, the future looks even brighter for the border city. Go ahead on, Laredo!

In closing, I will leave you with my favorite sailor's prayer. I don't know the poet who wrote it but this is a beautiful poem; I hope you like it.

O Master Sailor of the sea,
I bid Thee Sir come sail with me.
You know the course that I must take,
You know the land that lies await,
For conquering sailors of the sea
O Master Sailor, sail with me.

O Master Sailor, weary I grow,
I want so hard the way to know.
I have not sailed this sea before, nor do I know the oceans roar.
O Master Sailor of the sea
I bid thee Sir, my compass be.

Guide me to that blessed land,
O steer my ship with steady hand.
O keep me from the dangerous shoal,
Help me onward toward the goal.
O Master Sailor of the sea,
I pray thee, Sir, my Helmsman be.

When the stormy waves too high,
And my heart fears that I should die,
Then shall I see my bow before,
The blessed lighthouse on the shore.
Then all my thanks shall be to Thee
For, O Master Sailor, You sailed with me.